Houghton Mifflin
Mathematics

Practice

4

HOUGHTON MIFFLIN

BOSTON • MORRIS PLAINS, NJ

California • Colorado • Georgia • Illinois • New Jersey • Texas

Contents

Name _____ Date _____

Addition Properties

Example
$438 + 0 = \mathbf{438}$

Find each sum.

1. $6 + (14 + 17) = $ _____

2. $93 + 28 = $ _____

3. $36 + 93 = $ _____

4. $(45 + 5) + 16 = $ _____

5. $15 + 76 = $ _____

Complete each number sentence.
Tell which property of addition you used.

6. $22 + 88 = $ _____ $ + 22$

_____

7. $3 + (5 + 8) = (3 + $ _____ $) + 8$

_____

8. $67 + 0 = $ _____

_____

9. $(45 + 73) + 39 = 45 + (73 + $ _____ $)$

_____

10. $0 + 934 = $ _____

_____

11. $57 + 82 = 82 + $ _____

_____

Problem Solving • Reasoning

Use the table for Problems 12 and 13.

12. Are more children than teens pet owners? How can you use one of the properties of addition to help you decide?

_____

_____

Pet Owners			
	Children	**Teens**	**Adults**
Cats	24	56	35
Dogs	56	35	39
Gerbils	35	39	27

13. Do more people own cats than dogs? How can you answer without adding?

_____

_____

Name _____ Date _____

Add Whole Numbers

Example
745 + 362 **1,107**

Find each sum.

1. 559
+ 298

2. 837
+ 854

3. 1,345
+ 989

4. 3,662
+ 1,589

5. 634
+ 459

6. 2,075
+ 2,683

7. 11,989
+ 7,567

8. 23,574
+ 15,902

9. 63,629
+   774

10. 632 + 728

11. 1,067 + 493

12. 2,358 + 2,476

13. 37,328 + 4,063

14. 71,236 + 14,931

15. 55,408 + 39,277

Problem Solving • Reasoning

16. There is only one city in Delaware County, and that is Dunston. The population of Dunston is 65,490. There are 43,118 people living in Delaware County, but not in Dunston. What is the total population of Delaware County?

17. In 1999, 53,728 football fans attended the spring Kick-Off Fun Bowl. In 2000, 58,934 people attended. What was the total attendance for these two years?

Name _____ Date _____

Subtract Whole Numbers

Subtract. Add to check that your answer is correct.

Example
583
−148
435

1. 876
− 349

2. 3,992
− 475

3. 6,123
− 4,626

4. 8,825
− 7,736

5. 7,393
− 488

6. 4,821
− 4,653

7. 56,215
− 23,997

8. 39,9
− 28,

9. 88,458
− 27,399

10. 896 − 725

11. 695 − 438

12. 2,544 − 629

13. 4,772 − 2,936

14. 6,338 − 5,934

15. 8,772 − 5,385

16. 25,599 − 16,714

17. 75,129 − 24,662

18. 99,128 − 36,544

Problem Solving • Reasoning

19. There are 43,230 dogs in Jonesville. There are 55,911 cats. How many more cats than dogs live in Jonesville?

20. On Monday, 33,385 people watched the local news. On Tuesday, 33,975 people watched the news. How many fewer people watched the broadcast on Monday?

Name _____ Date _____

Estimate Sums and Differences

Round each number to the nearest ten.
Then estimate.

Example
76 + 22
80 + 20 = **100**

1. 68 − 32

_____

2. 191 + 57

_____

3. 4,033 − 692

_____

Round each number to the nearest hundred or dollar.
Then estimate.

4. 329 + 418

_____

5. $8.03 − $5.92

_____

6. 1,243 + 2,789

_____

7. 4,572 + 6,428

_____

8. 914 − 638

_____

9. 745 + 206

_____

10. $60.36 − $5.64

_____

11. 7,439 − 2,919

_____

12. 836 + 127

_____

13. 549 + 333

_____

14. $12.99 − $4.03

_____

15. 7,208 − 3,896

_____

Problem Solving • Reasoning

16. James had about 779 stamps in his stamp collection. His sister gave James her old stamp collection of 403 stamps. About how many stamps does James have now?

_____

17. The baker made 1,215 muffins last month. This month she baked 1,478 muffins. About how many muffins did the baker make in these two months?

_____

Name _____   Date _____

Problem-Solving Skill: Estimated or Exact Answers

Each summer the Whitfield Recreation Department offers summer classes for children. Classes are offered in three sessions. Enrollment for the first session is shown in the table.

Classes	Students Enrolled in First Session
Swimming	283
Martial Arts	192
Computer	217
Painting	95

Use the table. Decide whether you need an estimate or an exact answer. Then solve.

1. In the first session, about how many more students signed up for martial arts classes than enrolled in painting classes?

> **Think:** Is an estimate enough to solve the problem?

_____

_____

2. At the end of the session, each swimmer who passes a basic test receives a certification card. If all the swimmers enrolled in the class pass the test, how many certification cards will be needed?

> **Think:** Is the question asking for an exact answer?

_____

Solve. Use the table above. Use these or other strategies.

Problem-Solving Strategies

• Work Backward	• Guess and Check	• Write an Equation	• Use Logical Thinking

3. Twenty-four more students enrolled in the swimming class in the 2nd session than in the first session. How many students signed up for swimming in the second session?

_____

4. In the first session, 33 students did not pass the swimming test. How many students received their certification cards at the end of the first session?

_____

Name _____ Date _____

Subtract Across Zeros

Write each difference.

Example
705
−338
367

1. 601 − 298

2. 800 − 443

3. 509 − 197

4. 1,203 − 485

5. 4,808 − 1,236

6. 8,008 − 7,921

7. 21,070 − 12,993

8. 95,000 − 63,772

9. 80,030 − 25,094

10. 400 − 230

11. 930 − 390

12. 1,200 − 873

13. 3,078 − 1,345

14. 9,004 − 3,333

15. 7,701 − 2,999

16. 41,010 − 18,808

17. 98,000 − 76,121

18. 65,002 − 39,299

Problem Solving • Reasoning

19. Helen and John saved pennies for years. When they finally decided to put them in wrappers, it took days. Helen rolled 7,200 pennies. John rolled 6,893 pennies. How many more pennies did Helen roll?

20. The library in Middleton has 55,090 books on its shelves. The library in Brazleton has only 10,468 books. How many fewer volumes does the Brazleton Library own?

Name _____   Date _____

Problem-Solving Application: Use Operations

Use addition or subtraction to solve each problem.

1. The city of Jackson is studying 4 intersections to see if a traffic signal is needed. During one week, 47,458 cars passed through the intersections. Bill counted 9,936 cars passing through the Dun intersection. How many cars passed through the other 3 intersections?

Think: Do I need to find the total amount or a part of the total amount?

2. During that week, 16,901 cars were counted passing through the Benson intersection. During that same week, 8,047 cars passed through the Clarion intersection. How many cars passed through these two intersections during the week?

Think: Do I need to find the total amount, or a part of the total amount?

_____   _____

Solve. Use these and other strategies.

Problem-Solving Strategies

• Draw a Picture	• Write an Equation	• Solve a Simpler Problem	• Use Logical Thinking

3. There are 10,050 licenses for dogs in the city of Jackson. There are 6,428 licenses for cats. How many more dogs than cats are there in Jackson?

4. Jackson has 4 city parks. Three of the parks have 5 tennis courts. The fourth park has 8 tennis courts. How many tennis courts are there in all?

_____   _____

5. The Mayor of Jackson announced that the year 2003 would be the 150th anniversary of the founding of the city. In what year was Jackson settled?

6. On a summer day, 458 people visited the art museum in the afternoon, and 367 people visited in the evening. How many people visited that day?

_____   _____

Name _____ Date _____

Expressions and Equations

Example
$(30 + 5) + (14 - 7)$
$\quad 35 \quad + \quad 7$
$\qquad 42$

Simplify each expression.

1. $(23 - 6) + (14 + 12)$ **2.** $10 + (32 - 4)$

_____   _____

3. $(19 + 20) - (23 - 18)$ **4.** $(58 - 35) + 22$ **5.** $(47 - 15) - (21 - 17)$

_____   _____   _____

Complete using >, <, or = for each $\bigcirc$.

6. $8 + (95 - 22) \bigcirc (95 - 22) + 8$ **7.** $(55 - 6) + 3 \bigcirc 65 - (29 - 26)$

8. $23 + (17 - 13) \bigcirc 33 - (13 - 5)$ **9.** $(45 + 5) - 30 \bigcirc (67 - 27) - 20$

Write the missing number in each equation.

10. $35 = (25 + \underline{\qquad}) - 5$ **11.** $22 + 4 = (44 - \underline{\qquad}) + 3$

12. $(16 + \underline{\qquad}) + (14 - 7) = 18 + 22$ **13.** $18 = (48 + \underline{\qquad}) - 47$

Problem Solving • Reasoning

14. Jodie had a set of 24 drinking cups. Her cat broke 8 of them. Jodie went to a store to buy more cups but could only find 6 cups to match her set. Write an expression for the number of cups Jodie has now.

_____

15. Erika earned $25 baby-sitting. Then she earned $12 baby-sitting. She spent $20 on a gift for her sister's birthday. Write an expression for the amount of money Erika has now.

_____

Name _____ Date _____

Solving Addition Equations

1. Solve the equation $m + 7 = 12$. _____ Complete the tables below.

Start with the equation $m + 7 = 12$.

	Add this number to each side.	Write the new equation.	Solve the new equation.	Is the solution the same as the solution to $m + 7 = 12$?
2.	3		$m = 5$	yes
3.	6			
4.	10			

Start with the equation $m + 7 = 12$.

	Subtract this number from each side of the equation.	Write the new equation.	Solve the new equation.	Is the solution the same as the solution to $m + 7 = 12$?
5.	4		$m = 5$	yes
6.	5			
7.	6			

Name _____   Date _____

Equations With Two Variables

Complete each function table.

Example

$b = a - 6$

a	b
9	3
10	4
11	5

1. $n = s + 4$

s	n
1	
3	
	9

2. $z = 3 + x$

x	z
2	
4	
	9

3. $p = l - 2$

l	p
8	
6	
	2

Write an equation for each function table.

4.

c	a
18	12
15	9
12	6

5.

o	k
1	6
5	10
9	14

6.

f	d
6	2
8	4
10	6

7.

h	i
3	10
10	17
6	13

_____   _____   _____   _____

Problem Solving • Reasoning

8. Suppose that Brad is 11 inches taller than Kenton. Let b stand for Brad's height. Let k stand for Kenton's height. Write an equation that shows this relationship. Then use your equation to find Brad's height when Kenton is 46 inches tall.

9. Paul and Frank play 32 games of chess. Let p stand for the number of games won by Paul. Let f stand for the number of games won by Frank. Write an equation that shows this relationship. Then use your equation to find how many games Frank wins when Paul wins 14 games.

_____   _____

_____   _____

Name _____ Date _____

Multiplication Properties

Use the multiplication properties to help you find the products.

Example 5×0
Use the properties of Multiplication to solve the problem mentally.
When you multiply any number by 0, the product is 0.
So $5 \times 0 = \mathbf{0}$.

1. 4×1 **2.** 44×0 **3.** 0×15

_____   _____   _____

4. 1×64 **5.** 9×1 **6.** 18×1

_____   _____   _____

7. $(9 \times 1) \times 0$ **8.** $10 \times (1 \times 1)$ **9.** $(2 \times 2) \times 2$ **10.** $(6 \times 1) \times 1$ **11.** $2{,}000 \times 1$

_____   _____   _____   _____   _____

Solve each equation. Name the property that helped you.

12. $35 \times 0 = m$

_____

13. $2 \times 7 = t \times 2$

_____

14. $(6 \times 2) \times 3 = 6 \times (n \times 3)$

_____

15. $(6 \times r) \times r = 6$

_____

16. $(5 \times 3) \times v = 5 \times (3 \times 2)$

_____

17. $0 \times 22 = b$

_____

Problem Solving • Reasoning

18. Sheila wants to solve the equation 24×0. How can knowing the zero property help her determine the product?

_____

19. An item on a quiz gives two equations: 3×4 and 4×3. How can knowing the commutative property help you determine the products?

_____

Name _____ Date _____

Use Patterns to Multiply

Example
5 × 5
Count by 5s: 5, 10, 15, 20, 25.
So 5 × 5 = 25
5 × 10
Count by 10s: 10, 20, 30, 40, 50.
So 5 × 10 = **50**

Find each product.

1. 9
   × 1

2. 5
   × 7

3. 10
   × 3

4. 9
   × 5

5. 5
   × 1

6. 10
   × 2

7. 9 × 3

8. 5 × 1

9. 6 × 10

10. 9 × 7

_____   _____   _____   _____

11. 5 × 8

12. 5 × 0

13. 10 × 4

14. 3 × 5

_____   _____   _____   _____

Problem Solving • Reasoning

15. Diane is shopping for party favors. Each package of balloons contains 10 balloons. She needs 30 balloons. How can the patterns when you multiply by 10 help her figure out how many packages she needs?

_____

_____

_____

16. Steve wants to buy 27 whistles. Each bag of whistles contains 9 whistles. The clerk hands Steven 3 bags. How can patterns help Steven determine if the 3 bags will have enough whistles?

_____

_____

_____

Name _____   Date _____

Division With Remainders

Find each quotient and remainder.

Example
Find 19 ÷ 3.
Think of multiplication facts with products close to 19.
$3 \times n = 18$
$3 \times 6 = 18$
$18 = 19 - 1$
$19 \div 3 = n$
$19 \div 3 = $ **6 R1**

1. $2\overline{)13}$ **2.** $4\overline{)14}$ **3.** $7\overline{)25}$

4. $6\overline{)17}$ **5.** $9\overline{)47}$ **6.** $3\overline{)26}$

7. $6\overline{)29}$ **8.** $8\overline{)67}$ **9.** $5\overline{)39}$ **10.** $7\overline{)59}$ **11.** $6\overline{)58}$

12. 20 ÷ 7 _____   **13.** 66 ÷ 8 _____   **14.** 37 ÷ 6 _____   **15.** 14 ÷ 3 _____

16. 77 ÷ 9 _____   **17.** 21 ÷ 8 _____   **18.** 80 ÷ 9 _____   **19.** 47 ÷ 7 _____

Problem Solving • Reasoning

20. Elliot wants to store his 25 action figures in 3 shoe boxes. He wants to put the same number of figures in each box. How many figures will be in each box? How many figures will be left?

21. A popular mystery book series consists of 18 books. Adam and three of his friends want to share them equally. How many books will each person get? How many books will be left over?

_____

_____

Name _____   Date _____

Problem-Solving Skill: Multistep Problems

Solve.

1. For their play, the fourth grade needed 8 knights and 9 ladies. There were 27 boys and 28 girls in the class. How many times did they have to stage their play so every student got a part at least once?

> **Think:** What information do I have? What steps do I need to take to solve this?

_____

2. To stage their play, the students needed 6 parents to help. There were 32 jobs to do backstage. How many jobs did each parent have to do? Did some parents have to do more?

> **Think:** What are the questions? What steps do I need to take to find the answers?

_____

3. The students sold tickets to their play. They sold 60 adult tickets and 40 children's tickets. Adult tickets cost $2.00. Children's tickets cost $1.00. How much money did they make on the sale of tickets?

_____

4. To make their costumes, the students needed 2 different fabrics. They needed 10 yards of velvet, which cost $4.00 a yard. They also needed 20 yards of cotton, which cost $2.00 a yard. How much money did they need for all the fabric?

_____

Solve. Use these or other strategies.

Problem-Solving Strategies

• Make a Table	• Guess and Check	• Write an Equation	• Use Logical Thinking

5. The students needed $80 for fabric and $40 for supplies. If they made $160 selling tickets, did they have enough money? How much was left over?

_____

6. After the play, the class had a party. They made $40 on ticket sales, and someone donated another $25. They wanted to buy pizzas for $4 apiece. How many pizzas could they buy?

_____

Name _____ Date _____

Write and Evaluate Expressions

Example
7*n*
What does 7*n* mean?
7 × *n*
What is the value of the variable?
n = 7
So 7*n* = 7 × 7 = **49**

Evaluate each expression when *n* = 7.

1. 4 + *n* _____ **2.** *n* × 3 _____ **3.** *n* ÷ 7 _____

4. 19 − *n* _____ **5.** *n* × 9 _____ **6.** 28 ÷ *n* _____

7. *n* − 3 _____ **8.** 7 × *n* _____ **9.** 2*n* _____

10. 35 − *n* _____ **11.** *n* × 0 _____ **12.** *n* − 1 _____

Evaluate each expression when *r* = 4.

13. *r* ÷ 2 _____ **14.** 5*r* _____ **15.** *r* + 7 _____ **16.** 3*r* + 6 _____

17. *r* − 4 _____ **18.** 10 × *r* _____ **19.** 44 ÷ *r* _____ **20.** 6 • *r* _____

Evaluate each expression when *s* = 8.

21. 48 ÷ *s* _____ **22.** 3*s* _____ **23.** 17 − *s* _____ **24.** *s* + 3 _____

25. 2*s* + 4 _____ **26.** *s* × 7 _____ **27.** 8 ÷ *s* _____ **28.** *s* • 2 _____

Problem Solving • Reasoning

29. Jimmy and his friend Derek collect posters of rock stars. Jimmy has twice as many posters as Derek. Let *r* stand for the number of posters Derek has. Write an expression to show the number of posters Jimmy has.

30. Tara and Judy collect pens. Tara has 5 fewer pens than Judy has. Let *n* stand for the number of pens Judy has. Write an expression to show the number of pens Tara has.

Name _____   Date _____

Write and Solve Equations

Example
$5c = 45$
Solve
$5 \times \blacksquare = 45$
$\blacksquare = 45 \div 5$
$9 = 45 \div 5$
So $c = \mathbf{9}$.

Solve each equation. Check the solution.

1. $8p = 64$ _____

2. $s = 14 \times 2$ _____

3. $9z = 72$ _____

4. $20 \div r = 4$ _____

5. $d = 32 \div 4$ _____

6. $45 \div w = 9$ _____

7. $8q = 56$ _____

8. $5p = 35$ _____

9. $20 \div m = 10$ _____

10. $28 = y \times 7$ _____

11. $6p = 42$ _____

12. $9c = 36$ _____

13. $49 \div 7 = x$ _____

14. $m = 9 \times 7$ _____

15. $60 = 6p$ _____

16. $t = 28 \div 7$ _____

Problem Solving • Reasoning

17. Tim has 7 more sheets of colored paper than Marie. He has 36 sheets in all. Let v stand for the number of sheets Marie has. Write an equation that will let you find how many sheets Marie has.

_____

18. John bought some packs of thumb tacks with 20 tacks in each package. He has 60 tacks. Let x stand for the number of packs. Write an equation that will let you find out how many packs of thumb tacks John bought.

_____

Name _____ Date _____

Problem-Solving Application: Using Patterns

Remember:
▶ Understand
▶ Plan
▶ Solve
▶ Look Back

Use this array to answer the questions below.

	Column 1	Column 2	Column 3	Column 4	Column 5	Column 6
Row 1	2	4	6	8	10	12
Row 2	4	8	12	16	20	24
Row 3	6	12	18	24	30	36
Row 4	8	16	X	X	X	X
Row 5	10	X	X	X	X	X

1. If the pattern in Row 4 continues, what number should the last X in Row 4 be?

Think: What is the pattern?

_____

2. How is each number in Row 4 related to the number of the column?

Think: What is the question? What do you know?

_____

3. Let c represent the number of the column. Write an expression that describes the pattern in Row 4.

_____

4. Let c represent the number of the column. Write an expression that describes the pattern in Row 5.

_____

Solve. Use these or other strategies.

┌─────────── Problem-Solving Strategies ───────────┐

• **Use a Table**   • **Write an Equation**   • **Guess and Check**   • **Use Logical Thinking**

└──┘

5. Notice that the columns have a pattern too. If the pattern in Column 6 continues, what number should the last X in Row 5 be?

_____

6. Let r represent the number of the row. Write an expression that describes the pattern in Column 6.

_____

Name _____   Date _____

Solve Multiplication Equations

Begin with this equation.	Solve it.	The solution:
$3z = 9$	$z = 9 \div 3$	$z = 3$

Use the same equation to complete the table below.

	Multiply both sides by this number.	Write the new equation.	Solve the new equation.	Are the solutions the same?
1.	4	$(4 \times \underline{}) \times z = 9 \times 4$ $12z = 36$	$z = 3$	yes
2.	6	$(6 \times 3) \times \underline{} = 9 \times 6$ $18z = \underline{}$		
3.	3	$(3 \times \underline{}) \times z = 9 \times 3$ $9z = \underline{}$		
4.	2	$(\underline{}) \times z = 9 \times 2$ $6z = \underline{}$		
5.	5	$(\underline{}) \times z = 9 \times 5$ $15z = \underline{}$		
6.	1	$(1 \times \underline{}) \times z = 9 \times 1$ $3z = \underline{}$		
7.	7	$(\underline{}) \times z = 9 \times 7$ $21z = \underline{}$		
8.	10	$(\underline{}) \times \underline{} = 9 \times 10$ $30z = \underline{}$		

Name _____ Date _____

Two-Step Functions

Example

$y = 3x + 4$

x	y
5	

$y = (3 \times 5) + 4$
$y = 15 + 4$
$y = \mathbf{19}$

Complete each function table.

$n = 5m + 9$

m	n
1. 3	
2. 8	
3.	39

$a = 4b - 9$

b	a
4. 4	
5. 10	
6.	11

$r = 8s - 36$

s	r
7. 8	
8. 6	
9.	52

$c = 3d + 20$

d	c
10. 5	
11. 1	
12.	47

$e = 4 + 5f$

f	e
13. 4	
14. 8	
15.	14

$g = 6h - 18$

h	g
16. 11	
17. 6	
18.	24

$j = k + 89$

k	j
19. 13	
20. 48	
21.	140

$p = 48 \div m$

m	p
22. 6	
23. 4	
24.	16

$a = 3z \times 9$

z	a
25. 2	
26. 4	
27.	27

$y = 100 \div x$

x	y
28. 4	
29. 20	
30.	10

$k = 9g - 22$

g	k
31. 4	
32. 8	
33.	59

Problem Solving • Reasoning

34. Sandra scored 8 points in her first basketball game. In every game after that she scored 5 points. Let g stand for the number of games and P for the total points she scored. Write an equation that shows the total points she scored.

35. The rental at a bowling alley is $8 per hour. Shoe rental is $4. Write an equation that shows how much Jake will spend to bowl 2 hours. Let T stand for the total amount and h stand for the number of hours.

Name _____ Date _____

Problem-Solving Strategy: Write an Equation

Remember:
► Understand
► Plan
► Solve
► Look Back

Use the Write an Equation Strategy to solve each problem.

1. Mrs. Roth makes flags at her shop. She sells small flags for $6 each. Mr. Westland orders 10 small flags. How much will his order cost?

   Think: Let *f* stand for the number of flags. What expression could you write to show the cost of the flags?

   _____

2. Mrs. Roth needs 3 yards of red nylon, 6 yards of gold nylon, and 2 yards of green nylon. Nylon fabric costs $3.00 a yard. How much will she spend for fabric?

   Think: How can you show the cost of the fabric?

   _____

3. It costs Mrs. Roth $6 to make a medium-sized flag. She wants to make $3 profit on each medium-sized flag. How much will she have to charge if a customer orders 30 flags?

   _____

4. Mr. Thomas orders 9 small flags at $6 apiece, 20 medium-sized flags at $9 apiece, and 5 large flags. His total order costs $309. How much did he spend for each large flag?

   _____

Solve. Use these or other strategies.

Problem-Solving Strategies

• Use a Pattern   • Write an Equation   • Guess and Check   • Use Logical Thinking

5. Mrs. Roth is making flags for a special order. She needs 15 yards of white nylon, 8 yards of red wool, and 12 yards of blue cotton. Cotton costs $4 a yard. Nylon costs $3 a yard. Wool costs $6 a yard. How much will she spend for all the fabric?

   _____

6. Mrs. Roth can cut 9 stripes for her flags from one yard of fabric. Her flag pattern calls for 36 stripes. If the fabric costs $7 a yard, how much will it cost Mrs. Roth to make one flag?

   _____

Name _____ Date _____

Problem-Solving Strategy: Find a Pattern

Use a pattern to solve these problems.

1. Mr. Evers's math class has a contest to solve the problem of the week. Bob won this week when he predicted the next two numbers in this pattern.
4   6   12   14   28   30

Think: How do I get from the first number to the second? How do I get from the second number to the third?

_____

2. Joan won the math contest last week when she found the solution to this problem. Predict the next two numbers after the first seven.
3   8   6   11   9   14   12

Think: How do I get from the first number to the second? How do I get from the second number to the third?

_____

3. Three weeks ago, no one solved the problem of the week. Can you? Here it is. Predict the next two numbers in this pattern.
7   4   8   5   10   7   14

_____

4. The problem for next week is to predict the next two numbers in the following pattern. What numbers do you predict?
1   2   4   5   7   8   10

_____

Solve. Use these and other strategies.

Problem-Solving Strategies

| • Write an Equation | • Use Logical Thinking | • Guess and Check | • Draw a Picture |

5. In 1999, there were 6,273 people living in Baytown. When the Census counted the residents of Baytown in 2000, there were 354 more people. How many people were living in Baytown in 2000?

_____

6. Julio went to the hobby store and bought a model for $6.98. He also bought some new paint so that he could paint the model when it was done. The paint cost $2.50. How much did Julio spend at the hobby store?

_____

Name _____ Date _____

Multiply Three-Digit Numbers by One-Digit Numbers

Find each product. Estimate to check.

Example
227
× 3
681;
700

1. 327 × 2

2. $1.92 × 4

3. 415 × 4

4. 631 × 5

5. 792 × 3

6. $1.81 × 7

7. 798 × 2

8. $6.19 × 5

9. 221 × 9

10. 633 × 8

11. 247 × 6

12. 818 × 3

13. 428 × 4

14. $2.73 × 3

15. 893 × 2

16. 172 × 4

17. 647 × 7

18. 384 × 8

19. 181 × 9

20. $5.61 × 6

21. 782 × 5

Problem Solving • Reasoning

22. Bob finished building 178 birdhouses in one month. If he worked at the same rate, how many birdhouses would Bob finish in 7 months? First solve the problem. Estimate to check.

23. Jill's team of workers can pack 428 cartons of green beans every day. How many cartons can they pack in 5 working days? First solve the problem. Estimate to check.

Name _____   Date _____

Multiply Greater Numbers

Find each product. Estimate to check.

Example				
1,917				
$\times$ 4				
7,668;				
8,000				

1.   2,268
$\times$ 2

2.   2,881
$\times$ 6

3.   3,112
$\times$ 5

4.   4,189
$\times$ 3

5.   4,396
$\times$ 5

6.   2,492
$\times$ 7

7.   5,382
$\times$ 3

8.   8,114
$\times$ 9

9.   7,489
$\times$ 8

10. 1,399 $\times$ 2

11. 3,962 $\times$ 2

12. 5,311 $\times$ 8

13. 4,292 $\times$ 6

14. 7,129 $\times$ 7

Problem Solving • Reasoning

15. Joe visits his friend Sam 3 times every year. It is 1,176 miles one way from Joe's house to Sam's. How many miles does Joe travel in a year in the three round trips to Sam's?

16. The Jolly Cereal company produces 6,743 box of Yummies breakfast cereal every week. How many boxes of Yummies do they produce every in 9 weeks?

Name _____ Date _____

Multiply With Zeros

Multiply. Estimate to check.

Example
206
$\times$ 2
412; 400

1. 108
$\times$ 5

2. 504
$\times$ 8

3. 308
$\times$ 7

4. 409
$\times$ 3

5. 1,067
$\times$ 4

6. 2,308
$\times$ 9

7. 5,008
$\times$ 6

8. 7,025
$\times$ 7

9. 4,038
$\times$ 8

10. 307×5

11. $8,106 \times 3$

12. $9,003 \times 8$

13. $5,308 \times 5$

14. $6,098 \times 7$

Problem Solving • Reasoning

15. The course of the Shine Overland Bike Race is 306 miles long. The bicyclists travel the course 4 times to complete the Quad Trophy Race. How many miles do they complete for this race?

16. This year, 8,019 people came to the last State University basketball game. The same number of people come to each of the next 5 games. What is the total number of people who attended the 5 games?

Name _____ Date _____

Multiply Two 2-Digit Numbers

Multiply.

Example				
32	**1.** 82	**2.** 59	**3.** 74	**4.** 63
× 17	× 23	× 31	× 28	× 47
544				

5. 18 × 12   **6.** 24 × 39   **7.** 17 × 71   **8.** 32 × 68   **9.** 83 × 56

_____   _____   _____   _____   _____

Multiply. Use the Associative Property.

10. 16 × 40 = 16 × (_____ × 10)

= (_____ × 4) × _____

= _____ × _____

= _____

11. 48 × 50 = 48 × (_____ × 10)

= (_____ × _____) × _____

= _____ × _____

= _____

12. 33 × 80 = 33 × (_____ × _____)

= (_____ × 8) × _____

= _____ × 10

= _____

13. 72 × 90 = _____ × (_____ × 10)

= (_____ × _____) × _____

= _____ × _____

= _____

Problem Solving • Reasoning

14. There are 15 videos on each shelf in the video section of the library. There are 25 video shelves. How many videos are there in all?

_____

15. Dennis sells 47 computers each month. If Dennis sells the same number of computers each month, how many computers will he sell in one year?

_____

Name _____   Date _____

Multiply Three-Digit Numbers by Two-Digit Numbers

Find each product.

Example
123
× 50
6,150

1. 171
× 13

2. 215
× 28

3. 422
× 34

4. 391
× 72

5. 520
× 40

6. 208
× 63

7. 647
× 71

8. 812
× 21

9. 759
× 53

10. 60 × 117

11. 75 × 539

12. 38 × 904

13. 52 × 488

_____

_____

_____

_____

14. 438 × 16

15. 57 × 703

16. 369 × 18

17. 70 × 219

_____

_____

_____

_____

Problem Solving • Reasoning

18. Sue's Tomato Farm produces 825 pounds of tomatoes each week of the tomato season. The season is 12 weeks long. How many pounds of tomatoes does the farm produce in the season?

_____

19. The Posh Dress Factory makes 375 dresses each month. How many dresses are made in 3 years?

_____

Name _____   Date _____

Remember:
► Understand
► Plan
► Solve
► Look Back

Problem-Solving Application: Use a Pictograph

Abby was going with her family to visit her grandmother. To pass the time on the drive, Abby counted the colors of passing cars. The pictograph to the right represents the results of Abby's counting.

Car Colors

Green	🚗 🚗 🚗 🚗 🚗
Red	🚗 🚗 🚗 🚗 🚗 🚗 🚗 🚘
Blue	🚗 🚗 🚗 🚗 🚗 🚗 🚗 🚘
White	🚗 🚗 🚗 🚗 🚗 🚗 🚗 🚗 🚗 🚘
Yellow	🚗 🚗 🚗 🚗

🚗 = 10 cars

1. How many blue cars did Abby count?

Think: How do the number of 🚗 help me solve this problem?

_____

2. How many more red cars than green cars did Abby count?

Think: How many cars does a half of a 🚗 represent?

_____

3. For which color did Abby count 95 cars?

_____

4. How many cars did Abby count in all?

_____

Solve. Use these and other strategies.

Problem-Solving Strategies

• Use Logical Thinking   • Write an Equation   • Draw a Picture   • Find a Pattern

5. Janice and Mary have $65 total to spend on gift for their mother. Mary has $7 more than Janice does. How much money does each have?

_____

6. Paul is washing the windows of an office building. There are 6 floors. The first floor has 22 windows. Each of the other floors has 25 windows. How many windows does Paul wash in all?

_____

Name _____ Date _____

Modeling Division

Use play $10 and $1 bills to find the missing information.

	Amount in All	Number of Equal Groups	Amount in Each Group	Amount Left Over
	$12	2	$6	none
1.	$17	4		
2.	$21	5		
3.	$25		$5	
4.	$27		$6	
5.	$31		$5	
6.	$34	8		

Divide. Tell if there is a remainder.

7. Divide $26 into 3 equal groups. _____

8. Divide $18 into 6 equal groups. _____

9. Divide $33 into groups with $4 in each group. _____

Write About It

10. Five friends were given 15 one-dollar bills to share equally. Why is it possible for these 5 friends to share the bills equally?

_____

11. If the 5 friends were given 1 ten-dollar bill and 5 one-dollar bills, why would they have to regroup the ten-dollar bill to share the bills evenly?

_____

Name _____ Date _____

Two-Digit Quotients

Example
21 R2
3)65
−6↓
05
−3
2

Divide. Tell if there is a remainder.

1. 2)41 **2.** 5)50 **3.** 3)37

4. 4)81 **5.** 7)73 **6.** 2)89 **7.** 3)93

8. 3)64 **9.** 2)49 **10.** 5)59 **11.** 2)84

12. 82 ÷ 4 **13.** 67 ÷ 3 **14.** 28 ÷ 2 **15.** 79 ÷ 7

_____ _____ _____ _____

Problem Solving • Reasoning

16. Jill had 37 buttons. She gave each of her 3 brothers an equal number of buttons. How many buttons were left over?

17. There are 32 students in Simon's class. The teacher told students to form groups of 3. How many students could not form a group of 3?

_____ _____

Name _____ Date _____

Regrouping in Division

Example
14 R1
3)43
−3
13
−12
1

Divide.

1. 2)31

2. 5)60

3. 3)50

4. 4)71

5. 7)87

6. 2)83

7. 6)93

8. 9)91

9. 2)90

10. 5)91

11. 4)84

12. 75 ÷ 5

13. 83 ÷ 3

14. 57 ÷ 2

15. 39 ÷ 3

_____ _____ _____ _____

Problem Solving • Reasoning

16. Sonia, Sharon, and Al share a bag of pretzels. There are 40 pretzels in the bag. If they share all the pretzels evenly, how many are left over?

17. Trevor put all 54 of his CDs in 4 equal rows on his shelves. Any CDs that did not fit in the rows were put on his table. How many CDs were put on the table?

_____ _____

Name _____ Date _____

Problem-Solving Skill: Interpreting Remainders

When you solve a problem that has a remainder, you need to decide how to interpret the remainder. Sometimes the remainder is the answer. Sometimes you increase the quotient or drop the remainder to answer the question.

1. At Mary's Apple Farm, 89 apples are to be placed in small bags. Each bag holds 5 apples. How many bags are needed?

Think: Will the quotient or the remainder tell how many bags are needed?

_____

2. The next day, 74 apples are placed in the small bags. Each bag holds 5 apples. How many apples are not placed in the bag that is not full?

Think: Will the answer tell how many apples are in bags or how many are not in bags?

_____

3. There are 26 students in the class. Packages that contain 3 apples will be given to the class. How many packages of apples will be needed so that each student can have one apple?

_____

4. Mrs. Thomas's class will help pack apples in shipping boxes. The class is given 93 apples to pack. Each shipping box holds 8 apples. How many boxes can the class fill?

_____

Solve. Use these and other strategies.

Problem-Solving Strategies

| • Write an Equation | • Draw a Picture | • Find a Pattern | • Guess and Check |

5. Adam and Becky have $53 total. Becky has $9 more than Adam. How much money does each have?

_____

_____

6. Eddie collects football cards. He has 30 cards that he wants to display in equal rows. How many different ways can he arrange the football cards in equal rows so that there are no cards left over?

_____

_____

Name _____ Date _____

Mental Math: Divide Multiples of 10, 100, and 1,000

Example
6 ÷ 3 = **2**
60 ÷ 3 = **20**
600 ÷ 3 = **200**

Divide.

1. 12 ÷ 4 = _____
120 ÷ 4 = _____
1,200 ÷ 4 = _____

2. 20 ÷ 5 = _____
200 ÷ 5 = _____
2,000 ÷ 5 = _____

3. 180 ÷ 2 = _____

4. 900 ÷ 3 = _____

5. 140 ÷ 7 = _____

6. 250 ÷ 5 = _____

7. 240 ÷ 3 = _____

8. 160 ÷ 2 = _____

9. 640 ÷ 8 = _____

10. 420 ÷ 6 = _____

11. 240 ÷ 6 = _____

12. 1,400 ÷ 2 = _____

13. 2,700 ÷ 3 = _____

14. 7,200 ÷ 9 = _____

15. 1,200 ÷ 6 = _____

16. 2,800 ÷ 4 = _____

17. 1,800 ÷ 3 = _____

18. 3,600 ÷ 6 = _____

19. 8,100 ÷ 9 = _____

20. 2,100 ÷ 7 = _____

Problem Solving • Reasoning

21. Larry has a box of 1,200 paper clips. There is an equal number of the paper clips in 3 different colors: red, white, and black. How many black paper clips does Larry have?

_____

22. There are 240 students at Chris's school. The students are divided into 8 classes of equal size. How many students are in each class?

_____

Name _____ Date _____

Three-Digit Quotients

Example
275 R2
3)827
−6↓
22
−21↓
17
−15
2

Divide.

1. 2)361

2. 5)641

3. 3)495

4. 4)621

5. 7)837

6. 2)383

7. 6)923

8. 3)473

9. 2)932

10. 5)711

11. 4)924

12. 745 ÷ 5 _____

13. 875 ÷ 3 _____

14. 517 ÷ 2 _____

15. 559 ÷ 3 _____

Problem Solving • Reasoning

16. Jim used 695 beads to make a beaded bag. The beads came in packs of 5. How many packs of beads did Jim use?

_____

17. There are 271 students at Holly's school. The students lined up in 4 equal rows for the school photograph. Any students who could not fit in the rows sat at the front. How many students sat at the front?

_____

Name _____ Date _____

Place the First Digit of the Quotient

Example
58 R1
3)175
−15↓
25
−24
1

Divide. Then check your work.

1. 2)149

2. 5)381

3. 3)153

4. 4)169

5. 7)580

6. 2)133

7. 6)506

8. 3)161

9. 2)199

10. 5)368

11. 4)216

12. 206 ÷ 5
_____

13. 129 ÷ 3
_____

14. 154 ÷ 2
_____

15. 296 ÷ 3
_____

Problem Solving • Reasoning

16. Julia had 174 stickers. She sorted them into equal groups of animals, people, and words. How many of each group did she have?

_____

17. Valerie has 182 stickers. Pete has half as many stickers as Valerie. How many stickers do they have together?

_____

Name _____ Date _____

Divide Money

Example

$$
\begin{array}{r}
\$1.37 \\
3\overline{)\$4.11} \\
-3 \\
\hline
1\,1 \\
-\ 9 \\
\hline
21 \\
-21 \\
\hline
0
\end{array}
$$

Divide. Then check your work.

1. 2)$3.10

2. 5)$7.25

3. 3)$6.81

4. 4)$8.84

5. 7)$434

6. 2)$5.06

7. 6)$3.06

8. 3)$183

9. 2)$7.84

10. 5)$8.95

11. 4)$5.08

12. $8.92 ÷ 4

13. $4.29 ÷ 3

14. $194 ÷ 2

15. $7.74 ÷ 3

_____   _____   _____   _____

Problem Solving • Reasoning

16. Brett paid $3.80 for 5 raffle tickets at the local fair. What was the price of 1 ticket?

17. The fair raised $921. The money was given equally to 3 local charities. How much did each charity receive?

_____   _____

Name _____ Date _____

Zeros in the Quotient

Example
109 R1
7)764
−7↓↓
064
−63
1

Divide.

1. 2)412

2. 5)801

3. 6)365

4. 4)829

5. 7)984

6. 2)605

7. 6)618

8. 3)626

9. 2)820

10. 5)652

11. 4)360

12. 507 ÷ 5

_____

13. 496 ÷ 7

_____

14. 507 ÷ 2

_____

15. 316 ÷ 3

_____

Problem Solving • Reasoning

16. Bagels are sold in boxes of 6. If a store sells 624 bagels in one day, how many boxes were sold?

_____

17. The bagel store had 216 customers in one day. Half the customers arrived in the morning and half arrived in the afternoon. How many customers arrived in the morning?

_____

Name _____ Date _____

Problem-Solving Strategy: Work Backward

Work backward to solve the following problems.

1. Sean began painting his house on Monday. He worked 5 hours longer painting on Tuesday than he had on Monday. On Wednesday he worked 4 hours less than on Tuesday. On Thursday he painted 6 hours longer than on Wednesday. He painted for 11 hours on Thursday. How long did he paint on Monday?

Think: What information should you start with?

2. Mr. Brown made some lemonade for Spring Games Day at the school. When 4 gallons of the lemonade had been drunk, he made 6 gallons more. The children drank 4 more gallons. There were 2 gallons of lemonade left over at the end of the day. How much lemonade did Mr. Brown make at the start?

Think: What information should you start with?

3. On Monday, Bill checked out some books from the library. On Tuesday, he checked out 4 more books. On Wednesday, he returned 3 books. On Thursday, he checked out 2 books. On Friday, he returned all five books that he still had. How many books did Bill check out on Monday?

4. Gwen, Carla, Tod, and Dave are all reading the same book. So far, Gwen has read 10 pages less than Tod. Dave has read twice as many pages as Gwen. Carla has read 15 pages less than Dave. Carla has read 43 pages. How many pages has Tod read?

Solve. Use these and other strategies.

Problem-Solving Strategies

• Find a Pattern • Guess and Check • Draw a Picture • Work Backward

5. Look at the number pattern:
3, 7, 11, 15, 19, 23, 27, 31
What is the next number likely to be? Why?

6. Joellen bought a hammer and a box of nails. The nails cost $3. Joellen paid with a $20 bill. Her change was $2. How much did the hammer cost?

Name _____ Date _____

Divisibility Rules

Problems 1–4 are based on this group of numbers.

          110   70   35   95

1. Which numbers are divisible by 2?

_____

2. Which numbers are divisible by 10?

_____

3. Which numbers are divisible by 5?

_____

4. Which numbers are divisible by both 2 and 5?

_____

Complete this table. Use a check mark to show divisibility.

		10	28	35	70	88	50	95
5.	Divisible by 2	✔						
6.	Divisible by 5	✔						
7.	Divisible by 10	✔						

Problem Solving • Reasoning

8. Find a number between 21 and 39 that is divisible by both 2 and by 5.

_____

9. Find two numbers between 21 and 39 that are divisible by 5 but not divisible by 2.

_____

Name _____ Date _____

Prime and Composite Numbers

Write the factors for the numbers in the table below. Then, decide whether each number is prime or composite.

	Number	Factors	Prime or Composite
1.	31	1, 31	Prime
2.	32		
3.	33		
4.	34		
5.	35		
6.	36		
7.	37		
8.	38		
9.	39		
10.	40		

11. Which numbers from 41 to 50 are prime numbers?

_____

12. Which numbers from 41 to 50 are composite numbers?

_____

Problem Solving • Reasoning

13. Are there any prime numbers divisible by 2? Explain.

_____

_____

_____

14. John thought of a prime number between 1 and 10. Fred thought of a prime number between 20 and 30. The difference between the two numbers is 24. What were the two numbers?

_____

_____

Name _____ Date _____

Modeling Averages

Use counters to find the average of each set of numbers, or you may draw.

1. 2, 8 _____

2. 3, 5 _____

3. 5, 9 _____

4. 1, 2, 3 _____

5. 2, 3, 7 _____

6. 3, 5, 7 _____

7. 4, 6, 10, 12 _____

8. 4, 9, 6, 5 _____

9. 9, 10, 6, 11 _____

Use counters to find the missing number in each group.

10. Average = 4

_____, 6

11. Average = 7

4, _____

12. Average = 3

2, _____

13. Average = 6

_____, 5, 7

14. Average = 9

7, _____, 14

15. Average = 5

4, 9, _____

Write About It

16. Look at the numbers 9, 7, 10, 2, 11. Will the average of these numbers be closer to 2 or to 11? Explain your answer.

_____

_____

17. What operations could you use to find the missing number in a group if you know the average?

_____

_____

Name _____ Date _____

Find Averages

Example
4, 6, 7, 10

$$\begin{array}{r}5\\6\\7\\+10\\\hline28\end{array}\qquad 4\overline{)28}^{\,7}$$

Average = **7**

Find the average for each group of numbers.

1. 42, 22, 35

Average = _____

2. 102, 391, 89

Average = _____

3. $12, $31, $4, $17

Average = _____

4. 8, 18, 180, 24, 15

Average = _____

5. 7, 2, 9, 22

Average = _____

6. $70, $89, $153

Average = _____

7. 24, 28, 16, 19, 13

Average = _____

8. 1, 100, 4

Average = _____

Problem Solving • Reasoning

9. Dave, Max, and Frank bought kites. Dave's kite cost $14, Max's kite cost $23, and Frank's kite cost $17. What was the average cost of their kites?

_____

10. Greg saw three plays in one week. The lengths of the plays were 2 hr 30 min, 1 hr 15 min, and 2 hr 15 min. What was the average length of the plays that Greg saw?

_____

Name _____ Date _____

Estimate Quotients

Example
$$5\overline{)354} \rightarrow 5\overline{)350}^{\,70}$$

Estimate each quotient.

1. $8\overline{)635}$

2. $7\overline{)209}$

3. $2\overline{)176}$

4. $4\overline{)167}$

5. $9\overline{)191}$

6. $3\overline{)235}$

7. $5\overline{)462}$

8. $8\overline{)152}$

9. $7\overline{)500}$

10. $6\overline{)527}$

11. $6\overline{)111}$

12. $4\overline{)294}$

13. $3\overline{)155}$

14. $5\overline{)203}$

Problem Solving • Reasoning

15. Rick has 357 different marbles. The marbles come in six colors and there is approximately the same number of each different color. Estimate the number of each color marble Rick has.

_____

16. Glen and 2 of his friends spent $62 on marbles. Each person spent appoximately the same amount. Estimate how much each person spent on marbles.

_____

Name _____ Date _____

Divide Greater Numbers

Example

454 R1
5)2,271
−2 0↓
27
−25↓
21
−20
1

Divide. Check your work.

1. 2)3,645

2. 5)12,423

3. 3)8,120

4. 4)3,408

5. 7)6,590

6. 2)6,845

7. 6)$1,297

8. 3)9,032

9. 2)$1,880

10. 5)6,159

11. 4)29,402

12. 1,062 ÷ 5

13. $12,749 ÷ 3

14. 3,007 ÷ 2

15. 1,664 ÷ 3

Problem Solving • Reasoning

16. The population of Heather's town is 8,032. Half of the population is male. How many men live in Heather's town?

17. Shannon's almanac has 12,798 references. The references are divided equally into three volumes. How many references are in each volume?

Name _____ Date _____

Problem-Solving Application: Use Operations

Remember:
▶ Understand
▶ Plan
▶ Solve
▶ Look Back

Decide which operations to use to solve these word problems.

1. The Carson Main Library held a special 3-day exhibit of a local artist's work. On the first day, 8,233 people visited the exhibit. On the second day, 7,659 people visited. What was the average number of people who visited the exhibit each day?

   Think: What operations do I use to solve this problem?

2. The first day of the exhibit, 857 art items were checked out of the library. The next day, 634 items were checked out. The third day, 591 items were checked out. What was the average number of items checked out each day?

   Think: What operations do I use to solve this problem?

3. The art exhibit used 15 portable wall sections. Art was hung on each side of each wall. Eight wall sections had 6 large paintings on each side. Seven sections had 9 small paintings on each side. How many paintings were there in all?

4. To set up the exhibit, advertise it, plan it, and promote it took 25 library employees. Each worked an average of 7 hours on the exhibit. Altogether, how many hours did the employees work on the exhibit?

Solve. Use these and other strategies.

Problem-Solving Strategies

| • Draw a Picture | • Guess and Check | • Work Backward | • Write an Equation | • Set it up |

5. The total items checked out for the 3 days was an average of about 3,000 per day. The normal number per day is about 1,400. About how many times as great was circulation during the exhibit?

6. The coffee shop in the library lobby sold about 650 muffins a day for each of the 3 days. Muffins cost $2.00. How much money came in for muffins during the exhibit?

Name _____   Date _____

Inch, Half Inch, and Quarter Inch

Estimate the length of each object to the nearest inch. Then measure to the nearest inch, half inch, and quarter inch.

Example

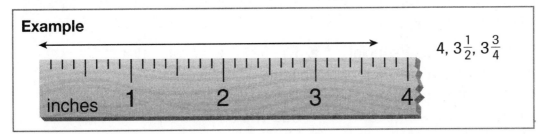

$4, 3\frac{1}{2}, 3\frac{3}{4}$

1.
_____

2.
_____

3.

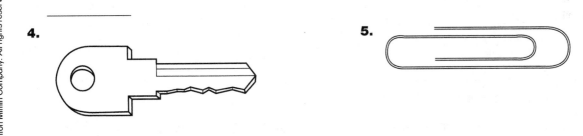

_____

4.

_____

5.

_____

Problem Solving • Reasoning

6. Draw a line that measures 2 inches when measured to the nearest inch, and measures $1\frac{1}{2}$ inches when measured to the nearest half inch.

_____

_____

7. **Write About It** Suppose an object measures 2 inches when measured to the nearest inch. What could it measure to the nearest half inch? Explain the possible answers.

_____

_____

Name _____ Date _____

Perimeter and Customary Units of Length

Find the perimeter of each figure.

Example

2 ft

1 ft ▭

1 ft + 2 ft + 1 ft + 2 ft = 6 ft
The perimeter is **6 ft.**

1. 30 ft
45 ft ▭

_____

2. 4 mi
8 mi ▯

_____

3. 7 yd
1 yd ▭

_____

4. 10 mi
25 mi ▯

_____

5. 3 yd
3 yd ▯

_____

6. 27 in.
10 in. ▭

_____

7. 12 in.
8 in. ▭

_____

8. 7 in.
7 in. ▯

_____

Problem Solving • Reasoning

9. A playground is 210 feet long and 180 feet wide. What is the perimeter of the playground in feet? in yards?

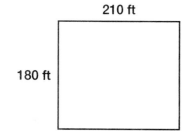

210 ft
180 ft

10. What is the perimeter of the triangle in feet? in inches?

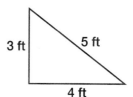

3 ft   5 ft
4 ft

_____   _____

Name _____ Date _____

Customary Units of Capacity and Weight

Find each missing number.

Example
4 qt = **8** pt
4 × 2 = 8

1. 2 qt = ___ c   **2.** 3 gal = ___ qt   **3.** ___ gal = 32 pt

4. ___ qt = 24 c   **5.** 7 gal = ___ qt   **6.** 13 pt = ___ c   **7.** ___ gal = 20 qt

8. ___ pt = 12 c   **9.** 14 qt = ___ pt   **10.** 4 gal = ___ c   **11.** 3 qt = ___ c

12. ___ gal = 72 pt **13.** ___ gal = 80 c **14.** ___ qt = 16 pt **15.** 5 gal = ___ qt

16. ___ lb = 3 T **17.** 2 lb = ___ oz **18.** ___ lb = 48 oz **19.** ___ lb = 6 T

20. 4 lb = ___ oz **21.** 96 oz = ___ lb **22.** ___ oz = 5 lb **23.** ___ lb = 5 T

Problem Solving • Reasoning

24. Kitt needs 10 cups of pear juice to make punch. What is the cheapest way he can buy the juice?

_____

25. Jenny bought 16 pint containers of pear juice. How much cheaper would it have been for her to buy the same amount of juice in gallons?

_____

Pear Juice Prices	
Item	Price
Pint	$.80
Quart	$1.50
Half Gallon	$2.75
Gallon	$5.00

Name _____   Date _____

Problem-Solving Skill: Too Much or Too Little Information

When a problem has too many facts, you must decide which facts are important. When a problem does not have enough facts, you must decide what facts are missing.

Yosemite Falls	
Upper Falls	1,430 ft
Middle Falls	675 ft
Lower Falls	320 ft

Use the information in the chart to solve each problem.

1. Are the Upper and Middle Falls over 2,000 feet high all together?

   Think: What information is extra?

   _____
   _____
   _____

2. Yosemite Falls is the world's 5th tallest waterfall. The world's tallest is Angel Falls in Venezuela. How much taller is Angel Falls than Yosemite Falls?

   Think: What information do I need?

   _____
   _____

Solve. Use these or other strategies. If not enough information is given, tell what information is needed to solve the problem.

Problem-Solving Strategies

- Write an Equation   • Guess and Check   • Draw a Picture   • Work Backward

3. Greg and Marcy hiked 1,040 yards in the morning. At the end of the day, they had hiked a total of 3,420 yards. How many yards did they hike in the afternoon?

4. Tiffany stayed at the Upper Falls for 23 minutes. She spent three times as long at the Lower Falls than at the Middle Falls. If she spent a total of 40 minutes at the Lower and Middle Falls, how long did she spend at each?

5. In the spring, about 2,400 gallons flow over Yosemite Falls every second. How many gallons flow over Yosemite Falls in 3 seconds?

6. Yosemite Falls is 2,425 feet tall. It is taller than the Empire State Building in New York City. How tall is the Empire State Building?

Name _____ Date _____

Centimeter and Millimeter

Estimate the length of each object to the nearest centimeter.
Then measure each object to the nearest centimeter.

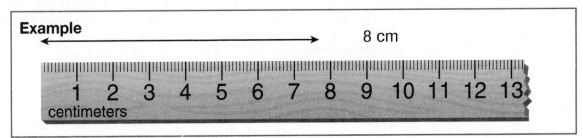

Example   8 cm

1.

   _____

2.

   _____

3.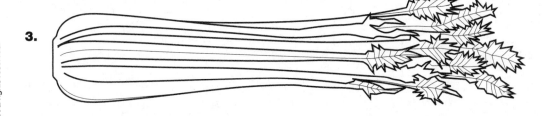

   _____

Problem Solving • Reasoning

4. Measure a side of the square to the
nearest centimeter. Suppose you use
this to estimate the perimeter of the
square. Would the actual perimeter of
the square be greater than or less than
the estimate?

5. Write About It Two different objects
both measure 4 cm to the nearest
centimeter. Suppose the objects were
placed together at their ends. Could
the objects measure a total of 9 cm to
the nearest centimeter? Explain.

_____

_____

Name _____ Date _____

Perimeter and Metric Units of Length

Find the perimeter of each figure.

Example

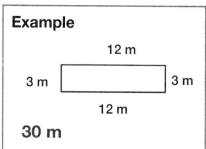

12 m
3 m   3 m
12 m

30 m

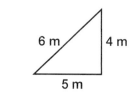

6 m   4 m
5 m

1. _____

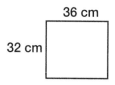

36 cm
32 cm

2. _____

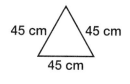

30 m
50 m   60 m
60 m

3. _____

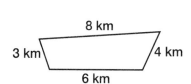

8 km
3 km   4 km
6 km

4. _____

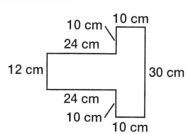

10 cm   10 cm
24 cm
12 cm   30 cm
24 cm
10 cm
10 cm

5. _____

45 cm   45 cm
45 cm

6. _____

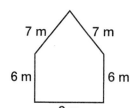

7 m   7 m
6 m   6 m
9 m

7. _____

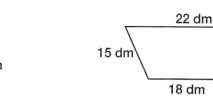

22 dm
15 dm   12 dm
18 dm

8. _____

Find each missing number.

9. 4 km = _____ m

10. _____ m = 60 dm

11. 7,000 m = _____ km

12. 500 cm = _____ m

13. 9 m = _____ cm

14. 800 mm = _____ cm

15. 7 cm = _____ mm

16. 15 km = _____ m

17. 9 m = _____ cm

Name _____ Date _____

Metric Units of Capacity and Mass

Find each missing number.

Example
2,000 g = **2 kg**

1. 5,000 mL = _____ L   **2.** 4 kg = _____ g

3. 3 L = _____ mL   **4.** _____ g = 8 kg   **5.** _____ mL = 9 L

6. _____ kg = 6,000 g   **7.** 15 L = _____ mL   **8.** 23,000 g = _____ kg

9. 12 L = _____ mL   **10.** 29 kg = _____ g   **11.** 35,000 mL = _____ L

Compare. Write >, <, or = for each ◯.

12. 500 g ◯ 5 kg   **13.** 2,000 mL ◯ 3 L   **14.** 3 kg ◯ 2,800 g

15. 2,500 mL ◯ 2 L   **16.** 42 kg ◯ 40,000 g   **17.** 5,000 mL ◯ 5 L

18. 13,000 g ◯ 12 kg   **19.** 7,000 g ◯ 7 kg   **20.** 5 L ◯ 5,500 mL

21. 20 g ◯ 20,000 kg   **22.** 9,400 mL ◯ 10 L   **23.** 48,000 mL ◯ 48 L

Name _____ Date _____

Problem-Solving Strategy: Make a Table

Use the table to solve problems 1-3.

1. The Polman School Band is going to the state band contest. Solo events go in grade level order. Fourth grade starts at 8:30 A.M. Each grade's solo events take $1\frac{1}{2}$ hours. When will the sixth-grade solos start?

Think: How can I organize this information in a table to solve the problem?

Time Solo Events Start		
4th Grade	**5th Grade**	**6th Grade**
8:30 A.M.	8:30 A.M. + $1\frac{1}{2}$ hours	5th grade start time + $1\frac{1}{2}$ hours

_____

2. Beverly plays flute in the fourth grade. She is the first flute solo, playing after 6 clarinet solos. Each solo takes 8 minutes. When will Beverly play?

_____

3. Josh plays the first saxophone solo in the fifth-grade. He follows 8 clarinet fifth-grade solos. If each solo takes 7 minutes, when will Josh play?

_____

Solve. Use these and other strategies.

Problem-Solving Strategies

• Make a Table   • Use Logical Thinking   • Guess and Check   • Work Backward

4. Dave has a length of rope 23 feet long. He needs 7 yards of rope to complete his playground swing project. Does he have enough rope to finish the project? Why or why not?

5. Barry has 43 paperback books in his room. Fourteen of them get wet and are ruined. Barry then buys 19 more paperback books. How many books does he have now?

Name _____   Date _____

Degrees Fahrenheit and Negative Numbers

Write each temperature.

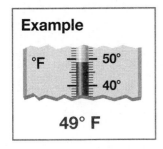

Example

49° F

1.

_____

2.

_____

3.

_____

4.

_____

5.

_____

6.

_____

7.

_____

Find the difference between the temperatures.

8. 37°F and 61°F

_____

9. 68°F and 104°F

_____

10. 27°F and 55°F

_____

11. 152°F and 191°F

_____

12. -12°F and 46°F

_____

13. -35°F and 73°F

_____

Problem Solving • Reasoning

14. Yesterday in Baytown the low temperature was 12°F. The day before that the low temperature was -3°F. How much warmer was it in Baytown yesterday?

_____

15. Chloe read the thermometer at 41°F. The wind made it feel as if it were 23°F. How much colder did the wind make the temperature feel?

_____

Name _____ Date _____

Degrees Celsius and Negative Numbers

Write each temperature.

Example

47° C

1.

_____

2.

_____

3.

_____

4.

_____

5.

_____

6.

_____

7.

_____

Find the difference between the temperatures.

8. 32°C and 81°C

_____

9. ⁻5°C and ⁻18°C

_____

10. 15°C and 43°C

_____

11. ⁻23°C and 64°C

_____

12. ⁻4°C and 92°C

_____

13. 67°C and 112°C

_____

Problem Solving • Reasoning

14. Tony put a thermometer in the water being heated in the pot. It read 72°C. How far below the boiling point is this?

_____

15. In the morning, the temperature was ⁻5°C. The temperature rose 12 degrees during the day and then fell 4 degrees that evening. What was the temperature in the evening?

_____

Name _____ Date _____

Equivalent Fractions

Multiply or divide to find the equivalent fraction.

Example

$\frac{2}{3} = \frac{2 \times 4}{3 \times 4} = \frac{8}{12}$

1. $\frac{2}{3} = \frac{2 \times 2}{3 \times \square} = $ _____

2. $\frac{2}{3} = \frac{2 \times 5}{3 \times \square} = $ _____

3. $\frac{4}{6} = \frac{4 \div 2}{6 \div \square} = $ _____

Is each fraction in simplest form? Write *yes* or *no*.

4. $\frac{5}{6}$ _____ **5.** $\frac{8}{10}$ _____ **6.** $\frac{2}{6}$ _____ **7.** $\frac{5}{9}$ _____

8. $\frac{3}{9}$ _____ **9.** $\frac{1}{8}$ _____ **10.** $\frac{3}{7}$ _____ **11.** $\frac{4}{20}$ _____

12. $\frac{2}{13}$ _____ **13.** $\frac{4}{8}$ _____ **14.** $\frac{3}{21}$ _____ **15.** $\frac{2}{14}$ _____

Write each fraction in simplest form.

16. $\frac{6}{18}$ _____ **17.** $\frac{4}{24}$ _____ **18.** $\frac{3}{30}$ _____

19. $\frac{5}{35}$ _____ **20.** $\frac{5}{25}$ _____ **21.** $\frac{2}{100}$ _____

Problem Solving • Reasoning

22. Sue read $\frac{2}{3}$ of the newest mystery book by her favorite author. Jack read $\frac{2}{6}$ of the same book. Did Sue and Jack read the same amount?

23. Erin and Kenyana ran laps around the running track at recess. Erin ran $\frac{6}{8}$ of a mile. Kenyana ran $\frac{3}{4}$ of a mile. Did they run the same distance?

_____   _____

Name _____   Date _____

Problem-Solving Strategy: Draw a Picture

Remember:
- ► Understand
- ► Plan
- ► Solve
- ► Look Back

The fourth grade students did surveys of groups of students in the school. Use the Draw a Picture strategy to solve each problem.

1. Of the first graders who were asked, $\frac{1}{6}$ like math best, $\frac{2}{3}$ like reading best, and 12 like science best. How many first graders were asked their favorite subject?

> **Think:** Into how many equal parts should the picture be divided?

_____

2. Of the second graders who were asked, $\frac{1}{2}$ like baseball best, $\frac{1}{8}$ like hockey best, and 30 like football best. How many second graders were asked their favorite sport?

> **Think:** Into how many equal parts should the picture be divided?

_____

3. Of the third graders who were asked, $\frac{2}{5}$ like pizza the best, $\frac{3}{15}$ like hamburgers best, and 18 like macaroni the best. How many third-graders were asked their favorite food?

_____

4. Of the fifth graders who were asked, $\frac{3}{7}$ like red best, $\frac{5}{14}$ like blue best, and 12 like green best. How many fifth graders were asked their favorite color?

_____

Solve. Use these other strategies.

┌───┐
│   **Problem-Solving Strategies**   │
│ • Draw a Picture │ • Make a Table │ • Write an Equation │ • Guess and Check │
└───┘

5. Ninety fourth graders voted about how to display the results of the surveys they took. Twice as many students voted to make a poster as voted to write a report. How many students voted to make a poster?

_____

6. The students spent 3 hours preparing the survey and 4 hours asking the questions. They spent 2 hours totaling the answers and 6 hours making the poster. How much time did they spend on the survey altogether?

_____

Name _____ Date _____

Fractions and Decimals

Example

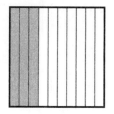

Fraction: $\frac{3}{10}$

Decimal: 0.3

Write a fraction and a decimal to describe each model.

1.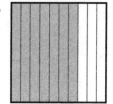

2.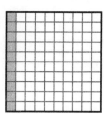

3.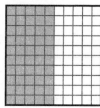

_____ _____ _____

**Use grid paper. Draw a model to show each fraction.
Then write each fraction as a decimal.**

4. $\frac{3}{10}$ _____   **5.** $\frac{7}{10}$ _____   **6.** $\frac{9}{10}$ _____   **7.** $\frac{2}{10}$ _____   **8.** $\frac{5}{10}$ _____

9. $\frac{6}{100}$ _____   **10.** $\frac{25}{100}$ _____   **11.** $\frac{48}{100}$ _____   **12.** $\frac{62}{100}$ _____   **13.** $\frac{85}{100}$ _____

**Use grid paper. Draw a model to show each decimal.
Then write each decimal as a fraction.**

14. 0.6 _____   **15.** 0.9 _____   **16.** 0.4 _____   **17.** 0.7 _____   **18.** 0.2 _____

19. 0.77 _____   **20.** 0.16 _____   **21.** 0.53 _____   **22.** 0.72 _____   **23.** 0.68 _____

24. Write About It How are $\frac{7}{10}$ and $\frac{70}{100}$ alike? How are they different?

25. Why is 0.03 less than 0.3?

_____

_____

_____

_____

_____

_____

Name _____ Date _____

Mixed Numbers and Decimals

Example

Mixed number: $2\frac{2}{10}$

Decimal: 2.2

Write a mixed number and a decimal for the shaded part.

1.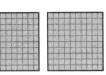

_____ _____

2.

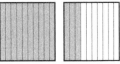

_____ _____

Write each mixed number as a decimal.

3. $8\frac{7}{10}$ _____

4. $19\frac{5}{10}$ _____

5. $35\frac{3}{10}$ _____

6. $3\frac{33}{100}$ _____

7. $26\frac{2}{10}$ _____

8. $18\frac{84}{100}$ _____

9. $6\frac{17}{100}$ _____

10. $27\frac{3}{10}$ _____

Write a decimal for each amount.

11. nine tenths _____

12. four and three hundredths _____

13. seventy-three hundredths _____

14. sixteen and two tenths _____

15. two and nineteen hundredths _____

16. forty-three hundredths _____

Problem Solving • Reasoning

17. Who had a time of forty-five and three-tenths seconds in the 100-yard dash?

_____

18. Which student had a time of approximately forty-nine seconds in the 100-yard dash?

_____

Times in the 100-yard dash	
Students	Times (seconds)
Mary	46.7
Jack	45.3
Pete	48.9
Will	42.6
Dana	44.8

Name _____ Date _____

Fractions and Decimal Equivalents

Example

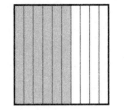

Six columns out of 10 are shaded.

As a fraction: $\frac{6}{10}$

As a decimal: **0.6**

Write a fraction and a decimal for the shaded part.

1.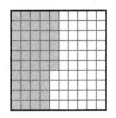

_____ _____

2.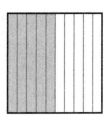

_____ _____

3.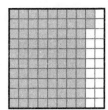

_____ _____

4.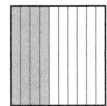

_____ _____

5.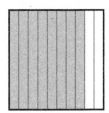

_____ _____

6.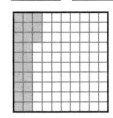

_____ _____

7.

_____ _____

8.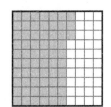

_____ _____

9.

_____ _____

10.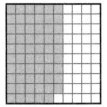

_____ _____

11.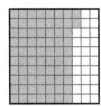

_____ _____

12.

_____ _____

13.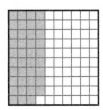

_____ _____

14.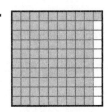

_____ _____

Problem Solving • Reasoning

15. In a bag of 10 marbles, 6 are blue, 3 are red, and 1 is white. Write a decimal that tells the part of the total of marbles that is each color.

_____

16. Suppose there are 100 marbles in the bag, and $\frac{3}{10}$ of them are white. The rest of them are blue. How many marbles are blue?

_____

Name _____   Date _____

Compare and Order Decimals

Example
2.6 ◯ 3.4
2 < 3
2.6 < 3.4

Compare. Write >, <, or = for each ◯.

1. 3.4 ◯ 1.9   **2.** 4.9 ◯ 5.6

3. 8.2 ◯ 9.1   **4.** 7.79 ◯ 7.29

5. 9.31 ◯ 9.31   **6.** 5.38 ◯ 5.83   **7.** 9.34 ◯ 3.90

8. 12.9 ◯ 12.6   **9.** 21.2 ◯ 12.1   **10.** 18.4 ◯ 16.2

11. 37.5 ◯ 73.5   **12.** 15.34 ◯ 15.43   **13.** 27.91 ◯ 26.83

Order the numbers from least to greatest.

14. 3.2, 3.9, 2.6, 1.5   **15.** 4.8, 3.2, 4.6, 8.4

_____   _____

16. 6.7, 9.6, 7.6, 7.9   **17.** 2.12, 2.19, 2.28, 2.21

_____   _____

18. 5.56, 5.25, 5.65, 5.52   **19.** 9.07, 9.80, 9.19, 9.38

_____   _____

20. 3.35, 3.53, 3.33, 3.52   **21.** 17.7, 7.71, 1.77, 71.1

_____   _____

Problem Solving • Reasoning

22. The high temperatures for each of the last five days were 75.3°F, 77.9°F, 84.6°F, 79.4°F, and 81.5°F. What is the order of the temperatures from greatest to least?

23. A decimal number with two digits is between 4.3 and 4.8 It is less than 4.71 and greater than 4.49. The digit in the tenths place is even. What is the number?

_____   _____

_____

Name _____ Date _____

Compare and Order Fractions, Mixed Numbers, and Decimals

Example
$3.2, 3\frac{4}{10}, 3.33, 3\frac{3}{100}$ The numbers from least to greatest are $3\frac{3}{100}, 3.2, 3.33, 3\frac{4}{10}$

Order the numbers from least to greatest.

1. $6.63, 6\frac{3}{10}, 6\frac{60}{100}, 6.36$

   _____

2. $4\frac{4}{100}, 4.44, 4\frac{4}{10}, 4.1$

   _____

3. $\frac{2}{10}, 2.2, 2\frac{2}{100}, 2.22$

   _____

4. $5.4, 5\frac{44}{100}, 5.54, 5\frac{4}{100}$

   _____

5. $8.2, 8\frac{8}{10}, 8.88, 8\frac{28}{100}$

   _____

6. $4\frac{44}{100}, 4.4, 4\frac{6}{10}, 4.64$

   _____

7. $9.1, 9\frac{11}{100}, 9.19, \frac{99}{100}$

   _____

8. $7\frac{73}{100}, 7.7, \frac{77}{100}, 7.77$

   _____

9. $6.36, 6\frac{3}{10}, 6.63, 6\frac{6}{100}$

   _____

10. $7\frac{9}{10}, 7.99, 9.79, 9\frac{9}{10}$

    _____

11. $2.23, 3\frac{2}{10}, 2.33, 3\frac{23}{100}$

    _____

12. $8.2, 8\frac{12}{100}, 8.21, 8\frac{22}{100}$

    _____

Problem Solving • Reasoning

13. During which month did it rain the most?

    _____

14. During which month did it rain the least?

    _____

Monthly Rainfall	
Month	Amount (inches)
February	$3\frac{33}{100}$
March	3.9
April	3.74
May	$3\frac{6}{10}$
June	$3\frac{3}{10}$

Name _____ Date _____

Problem-Solving Strategy: Find a Pattern

Use the Find a Pattern strategy to solve each problem.

1. At the county fair, one ride ticket costs $1.50. Two ride tickets cost $2.75. Three cost $4.00. Four cost $5.25. If the costs follow a pattern, what is likely to be the cost of six ride tickets?

Think: How does the amount change each time?

_____

2. At the fair, lemonade is sold in 4 oz, 8 oz and 12 oz glasses. The lemonade vendor says there's an even larger size, but she forgets what it is. The sizes follow a pattern. What size did she forget?

Think: What is the difference between each size and the next?

_____

Solve. Use these or other strategies.

Problem-Solving Strategies

• Work Backward	• Make a Table	• Find a Pattern	• Draw a Picture

3. Sarah is playing games at the fair. At the dart game, her third throw is a winner. At the basketball game, her fourth throw is a winner. At the milk bottle toss, each throw costs $1. How much will Sarah spend to win at the milk bottle toss, if her throwing has a pattern?

_____

4. On the way home, Mark notices a sign for the fair every 4 blocks. The signs follow a pattern. If Mark is 24 blocks from his home, how many signs will he pass by the time he gets home?

_____

5. The fair is open for 5 hours each day during the week. On Saturday and Sunday, the fair is open 7 hours each day. Pete works at the fair for three full days. He works a total of 17 hours. Did Pete work the fair on both Saturday and Sunday?

_____

6. The Ferris wheel is twice as tall as the roller coaster. The fun house is 23 feet shorter than the roller coaster. The water ride is 11 feet taller than the fun house. If the water ride is 25 feet tall, how tall is the Ferris wheel?

_____

Name _____   Date _____

Add and Subtract Decimals

Example
Check:
$\begin{array}{r} 9.83 \\ +8.20 \\ \hline 18.03 \end{array}$ $\begin{array}{r} 10 \\ +8 \\ \hline 18 \end{array}$

Add or subtract.

1. $\begin{array}{r} 4.4 \\ +8.7 \\ \hline \end{array}$

2. $\begin{array}{r} 33.3 \\ +56.6 \\ \hline \end{array}$

3. $\begin{array}{r} 6.48 \\ +7.35 \\ \hline \end{array}$

4. $8.4 - 6.2$

5. $9.3 + 4.5$

6. $6.72 - 4.31$

7. $32.9 + 15.6$

8. $\begin{array}{r} 44.83 \\ -21.54 \\ \hline \end{array}$

9. $\begin{array}{r} 64.05 \\ +83.36 \\ \hline \end{array}$

10. $\begin{array}{r} 75.23 \\ -49.15 \\ \hline \end{array}$

11. $\begin{array}{r} 14.48 \\ +19.93 \\ \hline \end{array}$

12. $17.2 + 18.9$

13. $9.2 - 7.5$

14. $44.41 + 83.32$

15. $67.38 - 43.97$

16. $\begin{array}{r} 29.91 \\ +30.77 \\ \hline \end{array}$

17. $\begin{array}{r} 83.39 \\ -27.65 \\ \hline \end{array}$

18. $\begin{array}{r} 36.36 \\ +77.77 \\ \hline \end{array}$

19. $\begin{array}{r} 54.89 \\ -32.01 \\ \hline \end{array}$

Problem Solving • Reasoning

20. Nick has $5.00 to spend on lunch. He bought a slice of pizza for $1.75, a glass of lemonade for $1.19, and an ice cream cone. If Nick has $0.51 left, how much did the ice cream cone cost?

21. On five math tests Janie scored 87.4, 93.6, 91.5, 85.7, and 89.9. What was the largest difference between any two scores?

Name _____ Date _____

Problem-Solving Application: Use Decimals

Remember:
► Understand
► Plan
► Solve
► Look Back

Solve each problem.

1. The distance from Canton, Ohio, to Cleveland is 30.7 miles. The distance from Cleveland to Sandusky is 32.9 miles. If you drove from Canton to Sandusky by going through Cleveland, how many miles would you drive?

Think: What operation should I use?

_____

2. If a person gets off a highway at the first exit, the toll is $1.25. If he gets off after 9 exits, the toll is $7.65. What is the difference between the tolls?

Think: Do I add or subtract?

_____

3. The drive from Pittsburgh to Baltimore takes 3.9 hours. It takes 9.7 hours to drive from Pittsburgh to Virginia Beach. How many more hours is the drive from Pittsburgh to Virginia Beach than from Pittsburgh to Baltimore?

_____

4. John's family drove from Pittsburgh to Virginia Beach, which took 9.7 hours. Then they drove from Virginia Beach to Baltimore, which took 3.2 hours. Then they drove home to Pittsburgh, which took 3.9 hours. How many hours did John's family drive altogether?

_____

Solve. Use these and other strategies.

Problem-Solving Strategies

• Work Backward	• Guess and Check	• Find a Pattern	• Act It Out

5. Sarah's family hikes on their vacation. The first day they hike 6.2 miles. The second day they hike 4.9 miles. The third day they hike 5.3 miles. How many miles did they hike altogether?

_____

6. On their three-day vacation, the family spent $74.63 the first day, $89.35 the second day, and $94.87 the third day. Altogether, how much money did they spend on their vacation?

_____

Name _____ Date _____

Round Decimals

Example

66.4

.4 < 0.5

66 is the nearest whole number for 66.4

Round each decimal to the nearest whole number.

1. 87.6 _____   **2.** 92.1 _____   **3.** 77.3 _____

4. 36.9 _____   **5.** 29.8 _____   **6.** 41.4 _____   **7.** 38.8 _____

8. 67.5 _____   **9.** 18.3 _____   **10.** 16.05 _____   **11.** 37.74 _____

12. 52.52 _____   **13.** 48.84 _____   **14.** 63.47 _____   **15.** 132.3 _____

Round each decimal to the nearest tenth.

16. 8.43 _____   **17.** 5.54 _____   **18.** 6.87 _____   **19.** 9.41 _____

20. 7.76 _____   **21.** 5.46 _____   **22.** 4.89 _____   **23.** 81.19 _____

24. 33.53 _____   **25.** 74.47 _____   **26.** 67.74 _____   **27.** 93.37 _____

Problem Solving • Reasoning

28. Martina bicycled for 8.4 miles on Friday, 13.8 miles on Saturday, 11.9 miles on Sunday, and 9.7 miles on Monday. On which two days did she bicycle for about 20 miles altogether?

_____

29. The grocery store has bags of flour which weigh 5.83 lb, 5.46 lb, 5.39 lb, 5.61 lb, and 5.48 lb. Which bags weigh less than $5\frac{5}{12}$ lb?

_____

_____

Name _____ Date _____

Estimate Decimal Sums and Differences

Estimate each sum or difference by rounding each decimal
to the nearest whole number. Then add or subtract.

Example		
7.3	rounds to	7
8.4	rounds to	8
+ 6.2	rounds to	6
sum: 21.9	estimate: 21	

1. 5.9
   7.7
   +9.2

2. $33.31
   + 65.54

3. 67.93
   +89.37

4. 4.8
   −3.9

5. 33.7
   −27.6

6. 85.77
   −68.45

7. 96.95
   −47.74

8. 53.36
   −29.91

9. $73.39
   + 36.47

10. 94.47
    +62.29

11. 87.33
    +28.83

12. $54.82
    + 87.74

13. 30.91
    +66.19

14. 97.38
    −34.76

15. $13.45
    − 9.67

16. 231.85
    −176.79

17. $748.32
    − 531.83

18. 978.84
    −683.49

19. 438.72
    +884.61

Problem Solving • Reasoning

20. In a music store, Jane finds one CD
    that costs $11.99. A second CD is on
    sale for $5.99. Jane has $20. Does
    she have enough to buy both CDs?

21. Tony practiced piano 4.75 hours one
    week. The second week, he practiced
    about 3.5 hours. About how many
    more hours did he practice during
    the first week?

Name _____ Date _____

Problem-Solving Skill: Choose a Computation Method

Use mental math, estimation, or paper and pencil.

1. Bill is earning money to buy a game. The game costs $49.97. One week he earned $11.76. The next week he earned $8.44. The following week he earned $13.02. And the fourth week he earned $16.75. Does he have enough money to buy the game?

Think: Is an estimate enough or is an exact answer needed?

_____

2. Alexis and four of her friends are running a lemonade stand. The first hour they make $2.57. The second hour they make $4.75. The third hour they make $3.83. They want to divide the money evenly. How much will each person get?

Think: Are the amounts easy to add without a paper and pencil?

_____

Solve. Use these and other strategies.

3. Paula made $12.50 by babysitting last week. She made $13.25 the week before. Two weeks ago she made $11.75. What was the average amount of money Paula made each week?

_____

4. Fred wants to know how much he has spent on his aquarium. He bought fish for $10.93. He bought fish food for $6.75. He bought chemicals for $4.37. About how much has he spent?

_____

Problem-Solving Strategies

- **Find a Pattern**
- **Work Backward**
- **Solve a Simpler Problem**
- **Write an Equation**

5. In one week Allie sells 5 of her paintings to classmates. She earns a total of $25. What is the average price of one of Allie's paintings?

_____

6. Bud has two dogs, two cats, and two hamsters. Anna has one dog, one cat, and one hamster. Bud spends about $5 each week to take care of his pets. About how much do you think Anna spends for her pets?

_____

Name _____ Date _____

Collect and Organize Data

Use the tally chart to answer Problems 1–3.

What is Your Favorite Pet?		
Pet	**Tally**	**Number**
Dog	𝍒 𝍒 𝍒 I	16
Cat	𝍒 𝍒 𝍒 II	17
Fish	𝍒	5
Hamster	𝍒 𝍒	10

1. How many people answered the survey question?

_____

2. What are the two least popular pets?

_____

3. List the pets in order, from least to most popular. _____

4. Use the list at the right to make a tally chart.

5. Look at your tally chart. What is the least popular subject?

_____

6. List the subjects from most to least popular.

_____

_____

What is your favorite subject at school?	
Mark	math
Leigh	science
Sarah	math
Latasha	English
Cara	history
Tom	math
Ellie	English
Mike	science
Leroy	history
Jake	history
Josh	math

Write About it

7. What are some ways that students might answer the question "What kind of lunch do you like to eat?"

_____

8. Can a survey tell you anything about the interests of the person who conducted the survey?

_____

Name _____   Date _____

Mean, Median, and Mode

Order the data from least to greatest. Find the range, mode, median, and mean. Then identify any outliers.

Example

4 7 5 7 17

4 5 7 7 17

range: **13**
mode: **7**
median: **7**
mean: **8**
outliers: **17**

1. 4 6 3 4 8

_____

range: _____
mode: _____
median: _____
mean: _____
outliers: _____

2. 19 6 21 19 20

_____

range: _____
mode: _____
median: _____
mean: _____
outliers: _____

3. 40 70 58 64

_____

range: _____
mode: _____
median: _____
mean: _____
outliers: _____

4. 1 1 10 2 1

_____

range: _____
mode: _____
median: _____
mean: _____
outliers: _____

5. 5 15 17 20 13 20

_____

range: _____
mode: _____
median: _____
mean: _____
outliers: _____

Problem Solving • Reasoning

6. Ron is keeping track of his scores in math class. On his math quizzes, Ron scored 80, 90, 95, 90, and 90. What was his median score? What was the mean score of the five quizzes?

_____

7. The students measured the height of the bean plants they were growing in science class. The heights were 12 cm, 15 cm, 18 cm, and 3 cm. What is the outlier in this set of data?

_____

Name _____ Date _____

Use Bar Graphs

Example

What is the total amount of money raised by the fourth graders at the bake sale and the candy sale?

$110.00

Use the bar graph to answer the questions.

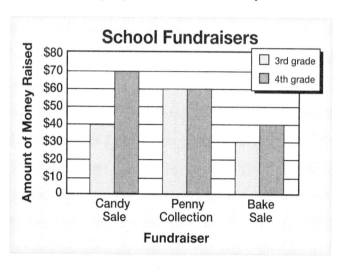

1. What was the median amount of money raised by the third graders?

_____

2. The fourth graders earned $130.00 doing which two fundraisers?

_____

3. At which fundraiser did the third and fourth graders earn the same amount of money?

_____

4. At which fundraiser did the third and fourth graders earn the most money combined?

_____

Problem Solving • Reasoning

5. At which fundraiser did the fourth graders earn $10.00 more than the third graders?

_____

6. At which fundraiser did the third graders earn twice as much as they earned at the bake sale?

_____

Name _____ Date _____

Problem-Solving Skill: Interpret a Line Graph

Sometimes you get information from a graph even though it does not have numbers or labels.

1. Why does the line stay the same height between point B and point C?

> **Think:** What does the height of the line represent?

_____

2. What point represents the most popular day to visit the museum?

> **Think:** What does the height of the line represent?

_____

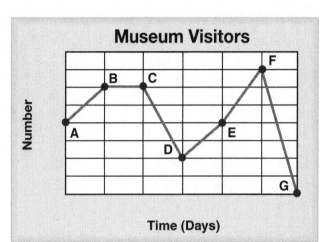

Museum Visitors

Number

Time (Days)

3. What point represents the day that the museum is closed?

_____

4. What do the 7 points on the graph represent?

_____

Solve. Use these or other strategies.

Problem-Solving Strategies

| • Use Logical Thinking | • Find a Pattern | • Choose the Operation |

5. Admission to the museum is $2.00 for adults and free for students. On Monday, 45 adults and 15 students visit. How much money will the museum charge in admissions?

_____

6. On Thursday, 4 people come to the museum the first hour it is open. During the second hour, 8 people come. In the third hour, 16 people come. If this pattern continues, how many people would you expect to come during the fifth hour?

_____

Name _____   Date _____

Read and Understand Line Graphs

Example
What was the temperature at 6:00 P.M.? **60°F**

The graph shows the temperature outside of Pablo's house throughout the day.

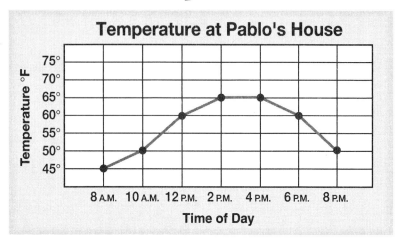

Temperature at Pablo's House

1. At which times of the day was the recorded temperature the same?

   _____

2. Between which two times of the day did the recorded temperature rise the most quickly?

   _____

3. Between which two times of the day did the temperature drop the most quickly?

   _____

4. What was the difference between the highest and lowest recorded temperatures on Pablo's graph?

   _____

Problem Solving • Reasoning

5. Suppose Pablo's temperature graph continued until 10:00 P.M. Would you expect the temperature at 10:00 P.M. to be lower or higher than the temperature at 8:00 P.M.? Explain.

   _____

   _____

6. Suppose the lowest temperature recorded on Pablo's graph was 60°F. How would the vertical axis of the graph be different?

   _____

   _____

Name _____ Date _____

Problem-Solving Strategy: Choose a Strategy

Remember:
► Understand
► Plan
► Solve
► Look Back

Sometimes you can solve a problem in more than one way.

1. There were 100 students and 20 adults on a trip to the zoo. Each bus can hold up to 55 people. What is the least number of buses they need to take?

Think: What equation could help me solve this problem?

_____

2. The students listened to a different song on the radio every 4 minutes they were on the bus. How many songs had they heard after 48 minutes?

Think: What operation could I use to help me solve this problem?

_____

3. The students each paid $1.00 to enter the zoo and $2.00 for lunch. How much money was paid altogether by the students for their zoo admissions and lunches?

_____

4. The students spent 2 hours looking at animals, went to two 1-hour zoo classes, and spent $\frac{1}{2}$ hour at lunch. How much time did they spend at the zoo altogether?

_____

Solve. Use these or other strategies.

Problem-Solving Strategies

• Use Logical Thinking	• Write an Equation	• Draw a Picture	• Guess and Check

5. Matt was first in line at the zoo. Steve was next to Matt and ahead of Marta. Joe was in front of Zach and behind Marta. What order are these students in from front to back of the line?

_____

6. The zoo is 75 miles from the school, and the bus can travel 50 miles in an hour. How many hours would it take to travel to the zoo?

_____

Name _____ Date _____

Probability and Outcomes

Look at the spinners. Write *certain, likely, equally likely, unlikely,* or *impossible* to describe the probability of landing on black.

Example

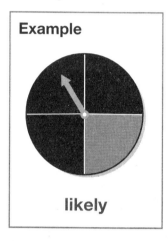

likely

1.

_____

2.

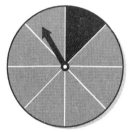

_____

3.

_____

4.

_____

5.

_____

Problem Solving • Reasoning

6. Mark was playing a game. Each player took turns spinning a spinner with the numbers 1 through 10 in equal-sized spaces. Is the probability of spinning a one-digit number on a turn *certain, likely, unlikely,* or *impossible*?

7. Susan picked out her socks in the dark this morning. In her drawer, she had 12 white socks and 2 blue socks. If she picks two socks, is the probability of her picking two blue socks *certain, likely,* or *unlikely*?

Name _____ Date _____

Find Probability

Suppose you draw one tile from this bag without looking. Use words and a fraction to write the probability of each outcome.

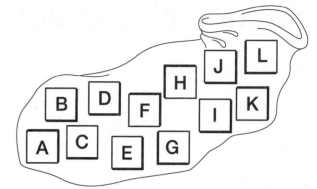

Example
B
$\frac{1}{12}$ unlikely

1. A or B or C

_____

_____

2. A vowel

_____

_____

3. D

_____

_____

Suppose you draw one tile from this bag. Use words and a fraction to write the probability of each outcome.

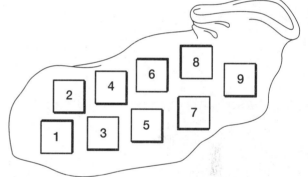

4. number less than 9

_____

_____

5. 1

_____

_____

6. 10

_____

_____

7. An even number

_____

_____

Problem Solving • Reasoning

8. Marla has a box with 4 orange buttons, 3 purple buttons, and one green button. Write a fraction showing the probability of picking an orange button.

_____

9. A piano has 88 keys. Show with numbers the probability of hitting a particular key if you shut your eyes and strike one key.

_____

Name _____ Date _____

Making Predictions

Make 10 cards like the ones shown.

1. Choose a card from the bag
without looking and put it back.
Repeat this step 25 times.

2. Predict how many times you
will pick the letter "t".

3. Record your results on a line plot.

4. Use your data to make a tally chart.

5. Use your data to make a bar graph.

i   r

a   i   m

t   c   h

e   t

Write About It

6. Which device makes your data easiest
to interpret, the tally chart, the line plot,
or the bar graph? Explain.

_____

7. What is the probability of picking the
letter "i" when you choose a card?
Suppose you picked a card from the bag
and put it back 50 times instead of 25
times. Would this change the probability
of picking the letter "i"? Explain.

_____

Name _____ Date _____

Represent Outcomes

Use the tree diagram for problems 1–3.

Example
How many possible outcomes are there?
4

What Joe Will Do After School

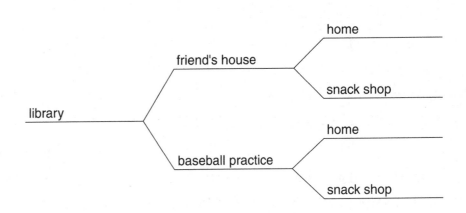

1. Write all of the possible outcomes.

_____

_____

_____

_____

2. Draw a new tree diagram to show what will happen if it rains and baseball practice is canceled.

3. How many possible outcomes are there if baseball practice is canceled?

_____

4. How many possible outcomes are there if the snack shop is closed?

_____

Problem Solving • Reasoning

5. Sue decided to read her book. After that, she will either ride her bike or roller blade, then eat pizza or tacos. Draw a tree diagram to show the possible outcomes.

6. Karen wants to do her art project either as a sculpture or a painting, colored red or blue. How many possible outcomes are there?

_____

Name _____ Date _____

Problem-Solving Application: Use Data and Probability

Remember:
► Understand
► Plan
► Solve
► Look Back

You can use the results of a survey to make predictions.

1. Twenty people named their favorite color for a car. The results are shown below.

Blue	Red	Black

Suppose 100 people were asked this question. How many do you think would choose red?

Think: Out of 20 people, how many chose red?

_____

2. Fifty students were asked to name their favorite school subject. The results are shown below.

Science	Math	English

Suppose 500 students were asked this question. How many do you think would choose math?

Think: Out of 50 students, how many selected math?

_____

Solve. Use these or other strategies.

Problem-Solving Strategies

| • Use Logical Thinking | • Write an Equation | • Draw a Picture | • Work Backward |

3. Six students worked together on a survey. Three of the students surveyed 15 people each. Two students surveyed 10 people each. One student surveyed 5 people. How many people did the students survey altogether?

_____

4. The students spent 5 minutes surveying each person. How long did the entire survey take?

_____

Name _____ Date _____

Points, Lines, and Line Segments

Use words and symbols to name each figure.

<table>
<tr>
<td>

Example

C

Say: **point** C

Write: C

</td>
<td>

1.

Say: _____

Write: _____

</td>
<td>

2.

Say: _____

Write: _____

</td>
</tr>
</table>

Write *parallel, intersecting* or *perpendicular* to describe the relationship between each pair of lines.

3.

4.

5.

6.

_____   _____   _____   _____

Draw an example of each.

7. Line *XY*   **8.** Vertical line segment *AB*   **9.** Point *Y*

Problem Solving • Reasoning

10. Find and print two letters from the alphabet that contain perpendicular lines.

11. Write About It Name something that you see on your way to school or in your school building that shows intersecting lines.

_____   _____

_____   _____

_____   _____

Name _____ Date _____

Rays and Angles

Name each angle in three ways. Then write whether each angle
appears to be *acute, obtuse,* or *right*.

Example

∠R
∠QRS
∠SRQ
obtuse

1.

_____
_____
_____
_____

2.

_____
_____
_____
_____

3.

_____
_____
_____
_____

4.

_____
_____
_____
_____

5.

_____
_____
_____
_____

6.

_____
_____
_____
_____

7.

_____
_____
_____
_____

Problem Solving • Reasoning

8. Dan drew an angle with a vertex
labeled *R*. The sides were labeled
T and *P*. The angle was obtuse. Draw
an angle that might look like the
angle Dan drew.

9. Keesha drew a right angle. She
labeled the vertex *N*. She labeled the
sides *W* and *D*. Draw an angle that
looks like the angle Keesha drew.

Name _____ Date _____

Polygons and Quadrilaterals

Name each polygon. If the polygon is a quadrilateral, write all names that apply.

Example

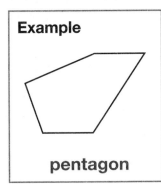

pentagon

1.

_____

2.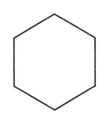

_____

3.

_____

4.

_____

5.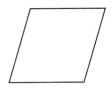

_____

6.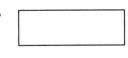

_____

7.

_____

Problem-Solving • Reasoning

8. Describe the difference between a rhombus and a parallelogram.

_____

_____

_____

_____

9. Describe the difference between a trapezoid and a rhombus.

_____

_____

_____

_____

Name _____ Date _____

Classify Triangles

Classify each triangle as *equilateral*, *isosceles*, or *scalene* and as *right*, *obtuse*, or *acute*.

Example

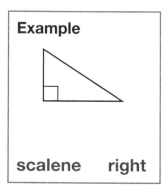

scalene   right

1.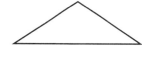

_____

_____

2.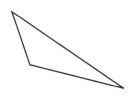

_____

_____

3.

_____

_____

4.

_____

_____

5.

_____

_____

6.

_____

_____

7.

_____

_____

Problem Solving • Reasoning

8. Chris drew a triangle in art class. Each side of her triangle was 3 inches long. Was her triangle scalene, equilateral, or isosceles?

_____

9. Nicole wants to draw a right triangle. One side has to be a right angle. What kind of angle can the other angles not be?

_____

Name _____ Date _____

Circles

Name the part of each circle shown by the line segment. Write
center, radius, diameter, or *none of these.*

Example	1. 	2.	3.

center

_____ _____ _____

4.   5.   6. 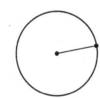 7.

_____ _____ _____ _____

Problem Solving • Reasoning

8. Ron draws a circle that has a diameter
of 32 inches. What is the measurement
of the radius of Ron's circle?

9. Is the minute hand on a clock more like
a diameter or a radius?

_____ _____

Name _____ Date _____

Congruent Figures

Do the figures in each pair appear to be congruent?

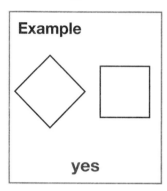

yes

1.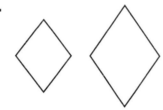

_____

2.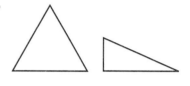

_____

3.

4.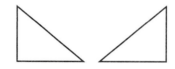

5.

_____ _____ _____

Problem Solving • Reasoning

6. Two triangles have perimeters of 12 inches. Are the triangles congruent? Write yes, no, or maybe. Explain your thinking.

_____

_____

_____

7. Two squares each have a perimeter of 12 inches. Are the squares congruent? Write yes, no, or maybe. Explain your thinking.

_____

_____

_____

Name _____ Date _____

Symmetry

Is the dashed line a line of symmetry? Write *yes* or *no*.

Example	1.	2.	3.
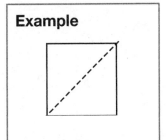 yes	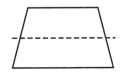		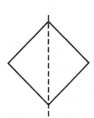

_____ _____ _____

Trace each figure on grid paper. Draw the line of symmetry.
Draw the other half of the figure on your grid paper.

4.

5.

6.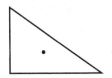

Trace each figure. Does the figure have rotational symmetry?
Write *yes* or *no*.

7.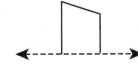

8.

9.

_____ _____ _____

Problem Solving • Reasoning

10. Print three letters from the alphabet that have a line of symmetry. Show the line of symmetry for each letter.

11. Does a circle always have rotational symmetry?

_____ _____

Name _____ Date _____

Problem-Solving Strategy: Use Models to Act It Out

Use these shapes to solve problems 1–4.

1. Use all of the shapes to make a square.

Think: How can I arrange or turn the pieces?

2. Use two of the shapes to make a rectangle.

Think: How can I arrange or turn the pieces?

3. Use three of the shapes to make a rectangle.

4. Use four of the shapes to make a different quadrilateral.

Choose a Strategy

Solve. Use these or other strategies.

Problem-Solving Strategies			
• Draw a Picture	• Make a Table	• Use a Model	•Work Backward

5. Draw a picture to show how two three-sided shapes could be put together to form a four-sided shape.

6. Draw a picture to show how a three-sided shape and a four-sided shape could be put together to form a four-sided shape.

Name _____ Date _____

Modeling Perimeter and Area

**Use grid paper to draw the figures described in each problem.
Then find the perimeter and area and record your answers
in the table.**

Shape	Perimeter	Area
Square A	20 units	25 square units
Square B		
Rectangle A		
Square C		
Rectangle B		

Example

Square A: length of sides:
5 units
The perimeter is 20 units.
The area is 25 units.

1. Square B:
length of sides: 3 units

2. Rectangle A:
length of sides: 1 unit, 2 units

3. Square C:
length of sides: 9 units

4. Rectangle B:
length of sides: 16 units, 2 units

Problem Solving • Reasoning

5. A square and a rectangle have the
same area. Will they always have the
same perimeter? Show an example.

6. A square and a rectangle have the
same perimeter. Will they always have
the same area? Show an example.

_____

_____

Name _____   Date _____

Use Formulas for Perimeter and Area

Find the perimeter of each polygon.

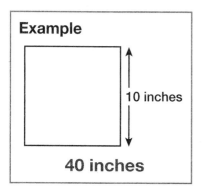

Example

10 inches

40 inches

1.

3 ft

2 ft

_____

2.
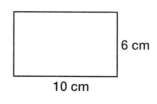

6 cm

10 cm

_____

3.
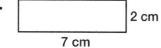

23 mi   2 mi

_____

4.
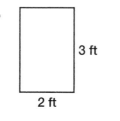

4 m   4 m

4 m

_____

5.

25 yd

20 yd

_____

Find the area of each polygon.

6.

6 mi

6 mi

_____

7.

2 cm

7 cm

_____

8.

1 foot

10 feet

_____

Problem Solving • Reasoning

9. Erin drew a rectangle that had a perimeter of 34 centimeters. The length of the rectangle was 15 centimeters. What was the width of Erin's rectangle?

_____

10. Ellen drew a square with an area of 25 square inches. What was the length of the sides of her square?

_____

Name _____ Date _____

Perimeter and Area of Complex Figures

Find the perimeter and area of each figure.

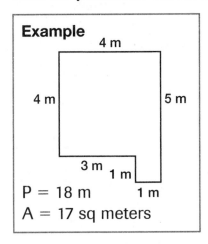

Example

4 m

4 m   5 m

3 m
1 m

1 m

P = 18 m
A = 17 sq meters

1.

4 mi   4 mi
4 mi   4 mi

8 mi   8 mi

12 mi

_____
_____

2.

10 ft

1 ft   1 ft
4 ft   4 ft

8 ft   8 ft

2 ft

_____
_____

3.

1 m 1 m
4 m

6 m   5 m

5 m

_____
_____

4.

5 yards

5 yards   6 yards

3 yards

1 yard
8 yards

_____
_____

5.

10 ft

2 ft
2 ft
8 ft   4 ft
2 ft

2 ft

10 ft

_____
_____

Problem Solving • Reasoning

Use the figure at the right for problems 6 and 7.

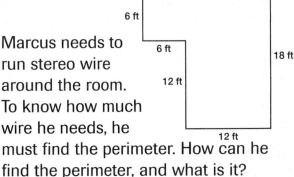

18 ft

6 ft

6 ft   18 ft

12 ft

12 ft

6. Marcus wants to buy carpet for the room shown in the figure. How can he find out how many square feet of carpet he needs, and how many does he need?

_____

_____

_____

7. Marcus needs to run stereo wire around the room. To know how much wire he needs, he must find the perimeter. How can he find the perimeter, and what is it?

_____

_____

_____

Name _____ Date _____

Problem-Solving Skill: Analyze Visual Problems

Remember:
► Understand
► Plan
► Solve
► Look Back

Choose the correct letter for the missing piece.

1.

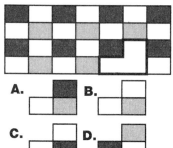

A. B.

C. D.

Think: Look at the columns to find the pattern.

2.

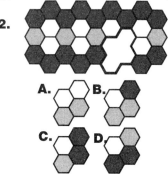

A. B.

C. D.

Think: Look at the rows to find the pattern.

_____   _____

Solve. Use these or other strategies.

Problem-Solving Strategies

| • Use Logical Thinking | • Find a Pattern | • Act it Out | • Draw a Picture |

3. Analyze A floor tile design has a pattern in which 4 out of every 9 tiles is white. In all, there are 81 tiles. How many tiles are white?

4. What is the next shape in the pattern likely to be?

Choose the correct letter for the missing piece.

5. _____

A. B.

C. D.

Name _____ Date _____

Solid Figures and Nets

Name the solid figure each object looks like.

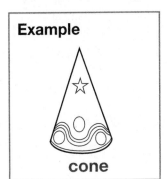

Example

cone

1.

_____

2.

_____

3.

_____

Name the solid figure that can be made with each net.

4.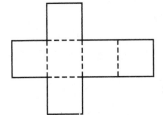

_____

5.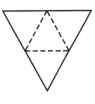

_____

6.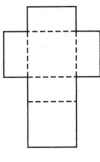

_____

7.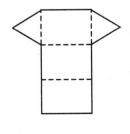

_____

8.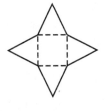

_____

Problem Solving • Reasoning

9. Write About It Describe 3 objects that look like rectangular prisms.

_____

_____

_____

10. Analyze A sphere can be rolled in any direction. A cylinder can be rolled in a straight line. How can a cone be rolled?

Use with text pages 498–500. **127**

Name _____ Date _____

Surface Area

Use the net to find the surface area of each solid figure.

Example

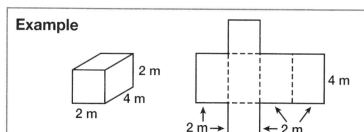

$8 \text{ m}^2 + 8 \text{ m}^2 + 4 \text{ m}^2 + 4 \text{ m}^2$
$+ 8 \text{ m}^2 + 8 \text{ m}^2 = 40 \text{ m}^2$

The area is 40 m².

1.

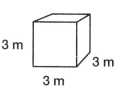
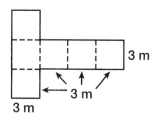

_____

2.

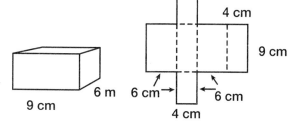

_____

3.

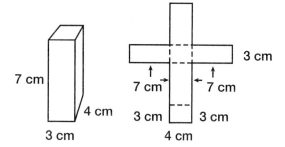

_____

Problem Solving • Reasoning

4. Each of the faces of a triangular pyramid has an area of 15 in.². What is the surface area of the pyramid?

_____

5. Analyze A rectangular box is 3 inches high, 10 inches wide, and 18 inches long. What is the surface area of the box?

_____

Name _____

Date _____

Volume

Find the volume of each figure.

Example

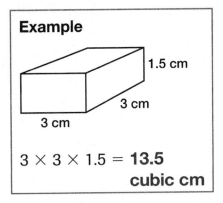

$3 \times 3 \times 1.5 = $ **13.5** cubic cm

1.

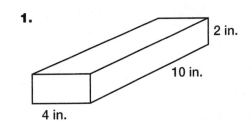

_____

2.

4 cm
4 cm
4 cm

_____

3.

18 m
9 m
6 m

_____

4.

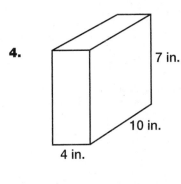

7 in.
10 in.
4 in.

_____

5.

5 m
11 m
9 m

_____

6.

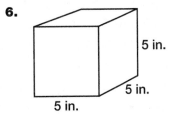

5 in.
5 in.
5 in.

_____

7.

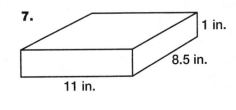

1 in.
8.5 in.
11 in.

_____

Problem Solving • Reasoning

8. A sandbox has dimensions of 1 ft by 5 ft by 6 ft. How many cubic feet of sand are needed to fill the sandbox?

_____

9. Analyze A tank needs to hold at least 500 ft³ of water. The bottom of the tank will be 9 ft by 9 ft. The tank should be a whole number of feet tall. How tall should the tank be?

_____

Name _____ Date _____

Problem-Solving Application: Using Formulas

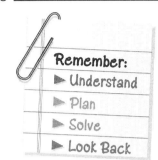

Remember:
► Understand
► Plan
► Solve
► Look Back

Jeremy is making a box to send a present to his grandmother. The box needs to be 12 inches long, 10 inches wide, and 5 inches high.

Use the information above to solve problems 1 and 2.

1. To find the amount of cardboard he needs, Jeremy needs to know the surface area of the box. What is the surface area?

   Think: How do I find the surface area of a rectangular prism?

   _____

2. What is the volume of the box Jeremy makes?

   Think: How do I find the volume of a rectangular prism?

   _____

Use these or other strategies.

Problem-Solving Strategies

• Draw a Picture • Write an Equation • Use Logical Reasoning

3. Jeremy bought 4 large sheets of cardboard and 3 small sheets of cardboard. The large sheets cost $1.17 and the small sheets cost $0.79. How much did the cardboard cost?

   _____

4. Jeremy is going to put an extra layer of cardboard in the bottom of the box. How many square inches of cardboard does he need for the extra layer?

   _____

5. What is the surface area of a shipping box that measures 12 inches on a side?

   _____

6. What is the volume of a shipping box that measures 12 inches on a side?

   _____

Copyright © Houghton Mifflin Company. All rights reserved.

Name _____ Date _____

Locate Points on a Grid Using Whole Numbers

Use the graph to the right for Exercises 1–15.

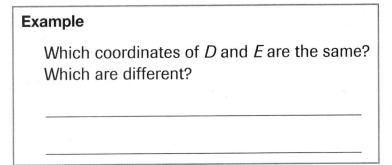

Example

Which coordinates of *D* and *E* are the same?
Which are different?

_____

_____
---

1. Does there exist any point whose coordinates
   are equal? How many such points exist?

   _____

Write the ordered pair for each point.

2. D _____   3. G _____   4. A _____

5. K _____   6. I _____   7. F _____

Write the letter of the point for each ordered pair.

8. (3, 0) _____   9. (0, 5) _____   10. (1, 2) _____

11. (5, 4) _____   12. (0, 3) _____   13. (7, 0) _____

Problem Solving • Reasoning

14. Write the letter of all points with *x*
    coordinate equal to 1.

15. Write the ordered pair of all points with
    y coordinate equal to 0.

_____   _____

Name _____   Date _____

Graph Ordered Pairs

Plot each point on the graph to the right.
Label the point with the letter.

1. *R* (5, 6)

2. *G* (6, 8)

3. *T* (6, 1)

4. *E* (2, 8)

5. *F* (4, 8)

6. *S* (5, 4)

7. *H* (8, 8)

8. *C* (1, 2)

9. *V* (4, 5)

10. *I* (7, 3)

11. *J* (8, 2)

12. *D* (9, 5)

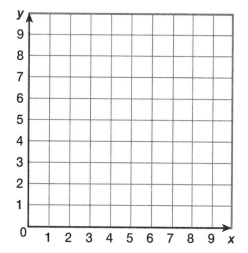

Problem Solving • Reasoning

Plot each point on the graph to the right.
Label the point with the letters.

13. Plot the points *A* (1, 6) and *B* (2, 2).
Connect the points to form a line.

14. Plot the points *X* (3, 3), *Y* (3, 1) and *Z* (6, 3).
Connect the points to form a triangle.

15. Plot the points *M* (3, 6), *N* (7, 6), *P* (7, 4) and
Q (3, 4). Connect the points to form a rectangle.

16. Plot *T* (6, 1). Connect *Z* and *T*, then *Y* and *T*.
What is *XYTZ*?

_____

17. Plot *C* (1, 2). Connect *A* and *C*, then *B* and *C*.
What coordinates of a point *L* would make
ACBL a rectangle?

_____

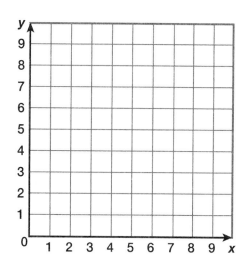

Name _____ Date _____

Graphs of Functions

Find the number of apples in 6 boxes.

Number of Boxes	Number of Apples
1	3
2	
3	
4	
5	

1. There are 3 apples in each box. Complete the table.

2. Write the pairs of data as ordered pairs. Record the number of boxes as the first coordinate and the number of apples as the second coordinate.

3. On the graph, plot the points named by the ordered pairs. Connect the points. Check that the points lie on a line.

4. Extend the line segment. Find the number of apples that would be in 6 boxes. _____

Problem Solving • Reasoning

Use the graph for Problems 5–8.

5. How many shoes are in 4 boxes? _____

6. How many shoes do you expect to be in 10 boxes? _____

7. Extend the line. Do you expect the point (10, 20) to be on the line? _____

8. Compare how many more shoes are in 7 boxes than in 3 boxes. _____

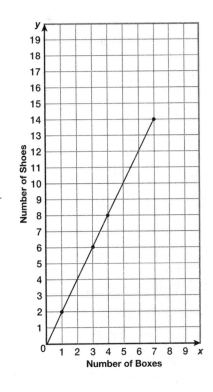

Name _____ Date _____

Problem-Solving Skill: Use a Graph

Solve. Use the graph at the right.

1. The manager of the grocery store was packing oranges in bags. If the manager used 5 bags, how many oranges did he pack?

> **Think:** Can you use one of the points marked to help you?

_____

2. If the manager packed 9 oranges, how many bags did he use?

> **Think:** How should you read the graph to find the number of bags used?

_____

3. How many oranges would you expect to be in 6 bags?

_____

4. How many bags would you need if you were to pack 21 oranges?

_____

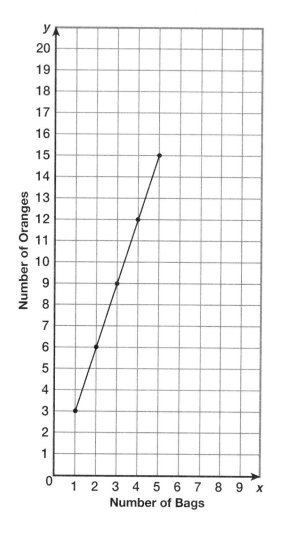

Solve. Use the graph above for Exercises 5–6. Use these or other strategies.

Problem-Solving Strategies			
• Guess and Check	• Find a Pattern	• Write an Equation	• Use Logical Thinking

5. The manager has 11 oranges that he wants to pack in bags. How many bags will he need?

_____

6. Let *y* stand for the number of oranges that the manager wants to pack. Let *x* stand for the number of bags needed. Write a rule to show a relationship.

_____

Name _____ Date _____

Integers

Example
2 hours before the movie starts
-2

Write the integer for each situation.

1. owe $5

_____

2. 12 degrees above zero

_____

3. behind 6 points

_____

4. 7 degrees below zero

_____

5. earn $4

_____

6. a balance of $14 in an account

_____

7. gain 6 pounds

_____

8. lose $8

_____

For Exercises 9-20 use the number line below.

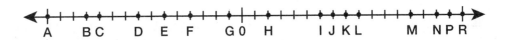

Write the integer for each letter on the number line.

9. E _____

10. J _____

11. N _____

12. B _____

13. I _____

14. R _____

15. F _____

16. L _____

17. G _____

18. M _____

19. H _____

20. D _____

Problem Solving • Reasoning

21. The temperature is 7 degrees below zero. What integer represents the temperature?

_____

22. The temperature is 42 degrees above zero. What integer represents the temperature?

_____

Name _____   Date _____

Identify Points on a Coordinate Plane

**For exercises 1–12 use the graph on the right.
Follow the directions. Write the letter and the
coordinates of each point.**

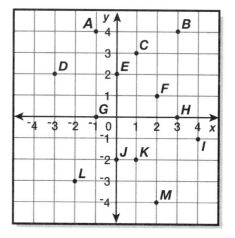

Example

Write the letter and the
coordinate of each point.
   Start at (0, 0).
   Move left 3 spaces.
   Then move up 2 spaces.

   D (-3, 2)

1. Start at (0, 0).
Move right 3 spaces.
Then move up 4 spaces.

_____

2. Start at (0, 0).
Move left 2 spaces.
Then move down 3 spaces.

_____

3. Start at (0, 0).
Move down 2 spaces.

_____

4. Start at (0, 0).
Move up 4 spaces.
Then move left 1 space.

_____

Name the letter of each ordered pair.

5. (2, 1) _____

6. (4, -1) _____

7. (0, 2) _____

8. (1, -2) _____

9. (-1, 0) _____

10. (2, -4) _____

11. (-1, 4) _____

12. (3, 0) _____

13. (1, 3) _____

Name _____ Date _____

Graph Ordered Pairs on the Coordinate Plane

Draw an *x*-axis and a *y*-axis on the grid. Number each axis
starting with 0 where the *x*-axis and *y*-axis cross.
Use your graph for the problems on this page.

Plot and label each point.

1. Point B ($^-1$, 4)

2. Point D ($^-6$, $^-2$)

3. Point F (5, $^-6$)

4. Point C (4, 2)

5. Point A ($^-5$, 3)

6. Point E ($^-2$, $^-4$)

7. Point J ($^-6$, 1)

8. Point G (4, 6)

9. Point I ($^-4$, $^-8$)

10. Point H (2, $^-2$)

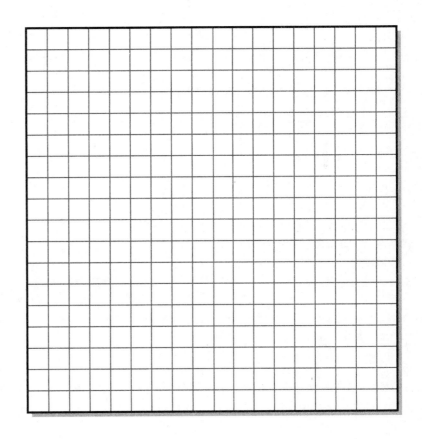

List all points that are:

11. above the *x*-axis

_____

12. below the *x*-axis

_____

13. to the right of the *y*-axis

_____

14. to the left of the *y*-axis

_____

Name _____ Date _____

Problem-Solving Strategy Choose a Strategy

Remember:
► Understand
► Plan
► Solve
► Look Back

Use a strategy to solve each problem.

1. Anne owes her brother $9. She borrowed $4 to buy a book. What integer represents how much Anne owes her brother now?

Think: Can I use a model to solve this problem?

_____

2. Notebooks are on sale. Each notebook is $1, but if you buy two, you get one free. How many notebooks can you get for $4?

Think: Can I make a graph to solve this problem?

_____

Solve. Use these or other strategies.

Problem-Solving Strategies

| • Make a Table | • Guess and Check | • Draw a Picture | • Use Logical Thinking |

3. James wants to send 3 packages by delivery service. Each costs $7. What is the total cost?

_____

4. Neil borrowed $5 each day for a week to buy kiwis. What integer represents how much he owes now?

_____

5. The volleyball team had 5 pizzas delivered after the game. Each pizza cost $7, and the delivery charge was $4. What integer represents how much they owe for the pizzas?

_____

6. Kim and Sarah played chess, and a winner was decided each time. They played 5 games in total. Sarah had one more victory then Kim. How many times did Kim win?

_____

Name _____ Date _____

Find Lengths on a Coordinate Plane

In problems 1–6 find the length of the line segment that connects each pair of points.

1. (4, ⁻2) (4, 4)

2. (5, 3) (5, ⁻1)

3. (⁻1, 2) (6, 2)

_____

_____

_____

4. (⁻2, 9) (⁻1, 9)

5. (7, ⁻4) (⁻1, ⁻4)

6. (⁻3, ⁻4) (⁻3, ⁻1)

_____

_____

_____

Use the grid on the right for problems 6–11. Graph each pair of points. Then find the length of the segment that connects each pair of points.

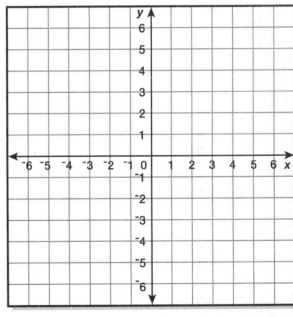

7. *A* (⁻3, 2)
  B (2, 2)

8. *C* (2, ⁻3)
  D (⁻3, ⁻3)

_____

_____

9. *E* (⁻1, 4)
  F (5, 4)

10. *G* (⁻1, 2)
  H (5, 2)

_____

_____

Problem Solving • Reasoning

11. The length of segment *AB* is 6 units. If *A* is named by (⁻4, ⁻3), and *B* is named by (■, ⁻3), then what are the possible values for ■ ?

12. A square is 4 units on each side. Two of the corners of the square are at points named by (⁻1, 2) and (3, ⁻2). Name the ordered pairs for the other two corners.

_____

_____

Name _____ Date _____

Problem-Solving Application: Use a Graph

Solve. Use the graph at right.

1. How much will it cost to rent 3 video tapes for a day?

   Think: Is the information you need on the graph?

   _____

2. How much will it cost to rent 7 video tapes for a day?

   Think: Can you extend the line to help find the answer?

   _____

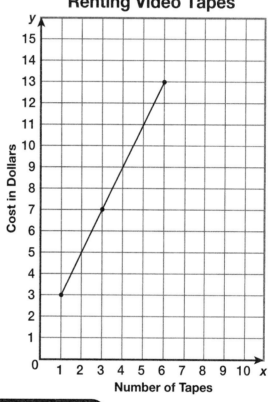

Daily Cost of Renting Video Tapes

Use the graph for Exercises 3–6. Choose any strategy to solve.

Problem-Solving Strategies

• Draw a Picture	• Find a Pattern	• Write an Equation	• Use Logical Thinking

3. How much will it cost to rent 9 video tapes for a day?

   _____

4. How many videos can you rent for one day for $17?

   _____

5. Let x stand for the number of video tapes. Let y stand for the cost of renting them for a day. Write a rule to show a relationship.

   _____

6. Use your rule from Problem 5. How much will it cost to rent 14 video tapes for a day?

   _____

Name _____ Date _____

Mental Math: Divide by Multiples of 10

Example

Find 36,000 ÷ 90.

Begin with a basic fact.
$36 ÷ 9 = 4$ ← basic fact
$360 ÷ 90 = 4$
$3,600 ÷ 90 = 40$
$36,000 ÷ 90 = 400$

Use basic facts to help you divide.

1. 54 ÷ 9 _____
540 ÷ 90 _____
5,400 ÷ 90 _____
54,000 ÷ 90 _____

2. 48 ÷ 8 _____
480 ÷ 80 _____
4,800 ÷ 80 _____
48,000 ÷ 80 _____

3. 63 ÷ 7 _____
630 ÷ 70 _____
6,300 ÷ 70 _____
63,000 ÷ 70 _____

4. 42 ÷ 7 _____
420 ÷ 70 _____
4,200 ÷ 70 _____
42,000 ÷ 70 _____

5. 35 ÷ 5 _____
350 ÷ 50 _____
3,500 ÷ 50 _____
35,000 ÷ 50 _____

6. 20 ÷ 4 _____
200 ÷ 40 _____
2,000 ÷ 40 _____
20,000 ÷ 40 _____

7. 45 ÷ 5 _____
450 ÷ 50 _____
4,500 ÷ 50 _____
45,000 ÷ 50 _____

8. 36 ÷ 6 _____
360 ÷ 60 _____
3,600 ÷ 60 _____
36,000 ÷ 60 _____

9. 30)1,500
10. 70)490
11. 60)30,000
12. 90)2,700

13. 40)24,000
14. 50)2,500
15. 80)320
16. 20)60,000

Problem Solving • Reasoning

17. The teacher has 120 apples to be divided among 40 students. How many apples does each student get? Explain how you got your answer.

18. The principal bought 500 pencils for the school. If the pencils come in boxes of 50, how many boxes of pencils did she buy? Explain how you got your answer.

Name _____ Date _____

One-Digit Quotients

Divide. Check your answer.

Example
Find 169 ÷ 42.   **Check your answer.**
$$\begin{array}{r} 4\,R1 \\ 42\overline{)169} \\ -168 \\ \hline 1 \end{array}$$ $$\begin{array}{r} 42 \\ \times\ 4 \\ \hline 168 + 1 = 169 \end{array}$$

1. $47\overline{)423}$ 2. $32\overline{)258}$ 3. $25\overline{)179}$ 4. $29\overline{)185}$

5. $24\overline{)213}$ 6. $54\overline{)499}$ 7. $32\overline{)296}$ 8. $65\overline{)129}$

9. $364 \div 46$ _____   10. $235 \div 35$ _____   11. $679 \div 73$ _____

12. $738 \div 82$ _____   13. $398 \div 67$ _____   14. $421 \div 57$ _____

Problem Solving • Reasoning

15. Cindy made 245 cookies for a fourth grade party. There are 49 students in the fourth grade. If shared equally, how many cookies can each student get?

16. Harry has a ball of kite string that is 120 meters long. If every kite needs 13 meters of string, how many kites can be flown using Harry's string?

_____

_____

_____

_____

Name _____ Date _____

Estimate the Quotient

Example
Estimate 64 ÷ 14
↓ ↓
60 ÷ 10 = 6
64 ÷ 14 is about 6.

Copy and complete each exercise. Use a new dividend and a new divisor to estimate.

1. 63 ÷ 16
↓ ↓
___ ÷ 20 = ___

2. 48 ÷ 13
↓ ↓
___ ÷ 10 = ___

3. 95 ÷ 23
↓ ↓
___ ÷ 20 = ___

4. 78 ÷ 36
↓ ↓
___ ÷ 40 = ___

5. 53 ÷ 12
↓ ↓
___ ÷ 10 = ___

6. 43 ÷ 21
↓ ↓
___ ÷ 20 = ___

7. 123 ÷ 18
↓ ↓
___ ÷ 20 = ___

8. 86 ÷ 27
↓ ↓
___ ÷ 30 = ___

9. 76 ÷ 15
↓ ↓
___ ÷ ___ = ___

10. 267 ÷ 34
↓ ↓
___ ÷ ___ = ___

11. 179 ÷ 62
↓ ↓
___ ÷ ___ = ___

12. 352 ÷ 47
↓ ↓
___ ÷ ___ = ___

13. 315 ÷ 38
↓ ↓
___ ÷ ___ = ___

14. 238 ÷ 78
↓ ↓
___ ÷ ___ = ___

15. 249 ÷ 52
↓ ↓
___ ÷ ___ = ___

16. 716 ÷ 82
↓ ↓
___ ÷ ___ = ___

17. 903 ÷ 96
↓ ↓
___ ÷ ___ = ___

Problem Solving • Reasoning

18. Doug has 117 stamps. He wants to divide them among 32 friends. About how many will each of his friends get?

_____

19. Jill has 182 hair ribbons. She wants to give ribbons to 24 friends. About how many will each of her friends get?

_____

Name _____ Date _____

Problem-Solving Skill: Multistep Problems

Solve.

1. Holly has 6 dozen eggs. She needs to divide them into cartons that hold 6 eggs each. How many of these cartons can she fill?

> **Think:** How many eggs does Holly have?

_____

2. Alec has 63 novels and 35 fact books. His bookcase has 5 shelves. How many books can he put on each shelf? Will there be any books left over?

> **Think:** How many books are there in all?

_____

Solve. Use these or other strategies.

Problem-Solving Strategies			
• Draw a Picture	• Make a Table	• Guess and Check	• Write an Equation

3. There are 275 seats in the theater. Seventy-five families, each with 4 people, buy tickets. How many shows will there have to be to seat everyone?

_____

4. Mr. Perez has an order for 12 dozen wooden cars. He has made 54 so far. How many more does he have to make?

_____

5. Amy, Beth, Cindy, and Dawn are standing in line. Amy is behind Dawn. Beth is not next to Cindy. Cindy is first in line. In what order are they standing?

_____

6. Ron gets 5¢ for every dandelion and 2¢ for any other weed he pulls out of the lawn. He pulls 53 dandelions and 126 other weeds. How much money will Ron get?

_____

Name _____ Date _____

Two-Digit Quotients

Example
Find 198 ÷ 12. **Check your answer.**

$$16 \text{ R}6$$
$$12)\overline{198}$$
$$-12$$
$$78$$
$$-72$$
$$6$$

$$16$$
$$\times 12$$
$$\overline{32}$$
$$16$$
$$\overline{192 + 6 = 198}$$

Divide.

1. $65)\overline{729}$
2. $25)\overline{849}$
3. $34)\overline{719}$

4. $52)\overline{958}$
5. $47)\overline{729}$
6. $96)\overline{4,416}$
7. $35)\overline{985}$

8. $63)\overline{1,679}$
9. $82)\overline{2,338}$
10. $47)\overline{3,396}$
11. $54)\overline{4,219}$

12. $1,392 \div 26$
13. $765 \div 42$
14. $648 \div 45$
15. $3,651 \div 94$

Problem Solving • Reasoning

16. One classroom can hold 34 students. The Worthington School District expects to have 7,582 students. How many classrooms will it need to hold everyone?

17. There are 2,583 children at Oak Elementary School. School buses can hold 62 children. How many buses will it take to carry all the students?

Name _____ Date _____

Adjusting the Quotient

Example

Find $46\overline{)418}$.

Estimate: $50\overline{)400}$ with 8 above.

$$\begin{array}{r} 8 \\ 46\overline{)418} \\ -368 \\ \hline 50 \end{array} \qquad \begin{array}{r} 9\ R4 \\ 46\overline{)418} \\ -414 \\ \hline 4 \end{array}$$

$50 > 46$

So 8 is too small.

Write *too large* or *too small* for each first estimate of the quotient. Then find the correct answer.

1. $64\overline{)123}$ with 2 above.

_____

_____

2. $26\overline{)251}$ with 10 above.

_____

_____

3. $34\overline{)121}$ with 4 above.

_____

_____

4. $72\overline{)525}$ with 6 above.

_____

_____

5. $46\overline{)529}$ with 10 above.

_____

_____

6. $84\overline{)418}$ with 5 above.

_____

_____

7. $29\overline{)186}$ with 5 above.

_____

_____

8. $32\overline{)298}$ with 10 above.

_____

_____

9. $68\overline{)559}$ with 7 above.

_____

_____

10. $94\overline{)452}$ with 5 above.

_____

_____

11. $86\overline{)729}$ with 7 above.

_____

_____

Problem Solving • Reasoning

12. Jenna is baking pies. Each pie has 8 slices. She needs to feed 296 people. She estimates that she will need to bake 30 pies. Is she right? Why or why not?

_____

_____

13. Joe is installing pipes that are 12 feet long. He has to lay 466 feet of pipe. He estimates that he will need 47 pipes. Is he right? Why or why not?

_____

_____

Name _____ Date _____

Problem-Solving Strategy: Solve a Simpler Problem

Boys' Polo Shirts	$8.99
Girls' Blouses	$7.99
Boys' Pants	$11.88
Girls' Skirts	$14.98
Boys' Tee Shirts	$7.77
Boys' Athletic Shoes	$56.55
Boys' Sweaters	$12.35
Boys' Socks	$1.95
Girls' Socks	$1.95
Girls' Tee Shirts	$7.77
Girls' Athletic Shoes	$42.88
Girls' Sweaters	$15.95

The Shopping Trip

Brett and Andrea are going shopping for school clothes. First they look at the prices in the newspaper. Then they go to their favorite department store. Here are the prices from the newspaper ad. Use them to help you answer the question.

1. Brett's mother says he can buy athletic shoes if he earns half the money himself. Brett makes $5.50 a week delivering newspapers. How long will it take him to earn enough money?

Think: How much money does Brett need to earn?

_____

2. Andrea is saving up to buy a sweater. She baby-sits for $2.50 an hour. How many hours will she have to baby-sit so that she can afford to buy herself a sweater?

Think: How much will Andrea earn in 2 hours? In 3 hours?

_____

Solve. Use these or other strategies.

Problem-Solving Strategies

• Draw a Picture   • Write an Equation   • Solve a Simpler Problem   • Guess and Check

3. Brett plans to buy athletic shoes, a polo shirt, pants, and 4 tee shirts. He has $110. Will he have enough money left over to buy socks?

_____

_____

4. Andrea also needs to buy socks for gym class. How much will she need if she wants to have a pair of socks for each day of the school week?

_____

_____

Name _____   Date _____

Zeros in Two-Digit Quotients

Example
Find 4,510 ÷ 50.
$\quad\quad$ **90 R10**
$50\overline{)4,510}$
$\quad -450$
$\quad\quad\quad 10$

Divide.

1. $24\overline{)729}$ $\quad\quad$ **2.** $83\overline{)1,675}$ $\quad\quad$ **3.** $49\overline{)4,418}$

4. $56\overline{)3,937}$ $\quad\quad$ **5.** $33\overline{)1,672}$ $\quad\quad$ **6.** $21\overline{)1,700}$ $\quad\quad$ **7.** $47\overline{)2,362}$

8. $62\overline{)1,870}$ $\quad\quad$ **9.** $36\overline{)2,901}$ $\quad\quad$ **10.** $74\overline{)2,993}$ $\quad\quad$ **11.** $85\overline{)3,479}$

12. $1,181 \div 13$ $\quad\quad$ **13.** $1,392 \div 23$ $\quad\quad$ **14.** $3,546 \div 59$ $\quad\quad$ **15.** $2,529 \div 36$

_____ $\quad\quad$ _____ $\quad\quad$ _____ $\quad\quad$ _____

16. $4,425 \div 55$ $\quad\quad$ **17.** $2,449 \div 61$ $\quad\quad$ **18.** $756 \div 37$ $\quad\quad$ **19.** $5,183 \div 74$

_____ $\quad\quad$ _____ $\quad\quad$ _____ $\quad\quad$ _____

20. $846 \div 14$ $\quad\quad$ **21.** $3,241 \div 46$ $\quad\quad$ **22.** $5,763 \div 72$ $\quad\quad$ **23.** $2,610 \div 29$

_____ $\quad\quad$ _____ $\quad\quad$ _____ $\quad\quad$ _____

Problem Solving • Reasoning

24. The class has collected 6,760 soda can tabs. They need to sort them, with 75 tabs in each box. How many boxes will they need? How many tabs are left over?

25. Brad has 333 decorations. He must put 16 decorations in each window. How many windows can he decorate? How many decorations are left over?

_____   _____

Name _____   Date _____

Problem-Solving Application: Use Operations

Remember:
► Understand
► Plan
► Solve
► Look Back

Solve.

1. Katie has joined a 10-week-long reading club. To get a prize, she must read 6 books each week. It takes her 5 hours to read one book. How many total hours will she have to spend reading to get a prize?

Think: What operation should I do first? What operation should I do next?

_____

2. The librarian is putting books on the shelves. She has 24 cartons of books. Each carton contains 24 books. She can fit 40 books on a shelf. How many shelves can she fill? How many books are left over?

Think: What operation or operations do I need to solve this problem?

_____

Solve. Use these or other strategies to solve each problem.

Problem-Solving Strategies			
• Draw a Picture	• Write an Equation	• Solve a Simpler Problem	• Guess and Check

3. There are 40 apples in every bushel. Ben makes 10¢ profit on every apple. If he sold 50 bushels of apples, how much profit would he make?

_____

4. In 2 hours a worker can pick 3 bushels of apples. There are 36 people who work 6 hours a day picking apples. How many bushels of apples can they pick in one day?

_____

5. You can pick a bushel of apples in 20 minutes. Is it better to get paid $2.25 for each bushel you pick or $6.25 for each hour you work?

_____

6. You are paid $2.25 for every bushel of apples you pick. You can pick 18 bushels a day. After 20 days, how much money will you have earned?

_____